EDWARD THE SECOND
(EDWARD II)

LECTOR HOUSE PUBLIC DOMAIN WORKS

EDWARD THE SECOND (EDWARD II)

CHRISTOPHER MARLOWE

ISBN: 978-93-5342-423-7

First Published: -

LECTOR HOUSE LLP
E-MAIL: lectorpublishing@gmail.com

EDWARD THE SECOND
EDWARD (II)

BY

CHRISTOPHER MARLOWE

CONTENTS

Page

ACT I.

- SCENE I. London, A Street. 1
- SCENE II. London, Near The King's Palace 7
- SCENE III. London, A Street 10
- SCENE IV. London, The New Temple.. 11

ACT II.

- SCENE I. A Hall In The Earl Of Glocester's Castle.. 24
- SCENE II. Tynmouth Castle. 27
- SCENE III. The Baron's Camp Before 35
- SCENE IV. Within Tynmouth Castle. 36
- SCENE V. Country Near Scarborough Castle 39

ACT III.

- SCENE I. Country Near Deddington. 44
- SCENE II. King's Camp, Near Boroughbridge, Yorkshire.. 45
- SCENE III. Another Part Of The Field, Boroughbridge. 50

ACT IV.

- SCENE I. London, A Street Near The Tower 54
- SCENE II. Paris.. 55

- SCENE III. London, A Room In The King's Palace.. 58

- SCENE IV. The Queen's Camp, Near Orwell, Suffolk. 60

- SCENE V. Near Bristol. 61

- SCENE VI. Within The Abbey Of Neath. 64

ACT V.

- SCENE I. Killingworth Castle. 69

- SCENE II. Westminster, A Room In The Palace. 74

- SCENE III. Near Killingworth Castle. 78

- SCENE IV. Westminster, A Room In The Pala. 80

- SCENE V. A Room In Berkeley Castle.. 84

- SCENE VI. Westminster, A Room In The Palace. 88

DRAMATIS PERSONAE

KING EDWARD THE SECOND.
PRINCE EDWARD, *his son, afterwards* KING EDWARD THE THIRD.
KENT, *brother to* KING EDWARD THE SECOND.
GAVESTON.
ARCHBISHOP OF CANTERBURY.
BISHOP OF COVENTRY
BISHOP OF WINCHESTER.
WARWICK.
LANCASTER.
PEMBROKE.
ARUNDER.
LEICESTER.
BERKELEY.
MORTIMER *the elder.*
MORTIMER *the younger, his nephew.*
SPENSER *the elder.*
SPENSER *the younger, his son.*
BALDOCK.
BAUMONT.
TRUSSEL.
GURNEY.
MATREVIS.
LIGHTBORN.
SIR JOHN OF HAINAULT.
LEVUNE.
RICE AP HOWEL.
ABBOT.
MONKS.
HERALD.
LORDS, POOR MEN, JAMES, MOWER, CHAMPION,
MESSENGERS, SOLDIERS, *and* ATTENDANTS.

QUEEN ISABELLA, *wife to* KING EDWARD THE SECOND.
NIECE *to* KING EDWARD THE SECOND, _daughter to
the *DUKE OF GLOCESTER.*
LADIES.

ACT I.

SCENE I. LONDON, A STREET.

Enter GAVESTON, *reading a letter.*

Gav. My father is deceas'd. Come, Gaveston,
And share the kingdom with thy dearest friend.
Ah, words that make me surfeit with delight!
What greater bliss can hap to Gaveston
Than live and be the favourite of a king!
Sweet prince, I come! these, thy amorous lines
Might have enforc'd me to have swum from France,
And, like Leander, gasp'd upon the sand,
So thou wouldst smile, and take me in thine arms.
The sight of London to my exil'd eyes
Is as Elysium to a new-come soul:
Not that I love the city or the men,
But that it harbours him I hold so dear,—
The king, upon whose bosom let me lie,
And with the world be still at enmity.
What need the arctic people love star-light,
To whom the sun shines both by day and night?
Farewell base stooping to the lordly peers!
My knee shall bow to none but to the king.
As for the multitude, that are but sparks,
Rak'd up in embers of their poverty,—
Tanti,—I'll fawn first on the wind,
That glanceth at my lips, and flieth away.

Enter three Poor Men.

But how now! what are these?

Poor Men. Such as desire your worship's service.

Gav. What canst thou do?

First P. Man. I can ride.

Gav. But I have no horse.—What art thou?

Sec. P. Man A traveller.

Gav. Let me see; thou wouldst do well
To wait at my trencher, and tell me lies at dinner-time;
And, as I like your discoursing, I'll have you.—

And what art thou?

Third P. Man. A soldier, that hath serv'd against the Scot.

Gav. Why, there are hospitals for such as you:
I have no war; and therefore, sir, be gone.

Third P. Man. Farewell, and perish by a soldier's hand,
That wouldst reward them with an hospital!

Gav. Ay, ay, these words of his move me as much
As if a goose should play the porcupine,
And dart her plumes, thinking to pierce my breast.
But yet it is no pain to speak men fair;
I'll flatter these, and make them live in hope. — [*Aside.*
You know that I came lately out of France,
And yet I have not view'd my lord the king:
If I speed well, I'll entertain you all.

All. We thank your worship.

Gav. I have some business: leave me to myself.

All. We will wait here about the court.

Gav. Do. [*Exeunt Poor Men.*
These are not men for me;
I must have wanton poets, pleasant wits,
Musicians, that with touching of a string
May draw the pliant king which way I please:
Music and poetry is his delight;
Therefore I'll have Italian masks by night,
Sweet speeches, comedies, and pleasing shows;
And in the day, when he shall walk abroad,
Like sylvan nymphs my pages shall be clad;
My men, like satyrs grazing on the lawns,
Shall with their goat-feet dance the antic hay;
Sometime a lovely boy in Dian's shape,
With hair that gilds the water as it glides
Crownets of pearl about his naked arms,
And in his sportful hands an olive-tree,
To hide those parts which men delight to see,
Shall bathe him in a spring; and there, hard by,
One like Actæon, peeping through the grove,
Shall by the angry goddess be transform'd,
And running in the likeness of an hart,
By yelping hounds pull'd down, shall semm to die:
Such things as these best please his majesty. —
Here comes my lord the king, and the nobles,
From the parliament. I'll stand aside. [*Retires.*

Enter KING EDWARD, KENT, LANCASTER, *the elder* MORTIMER,

the younger MORTIMER, WARWICK, PEMBROKE, *and* Attendants.

K. Edw. Lancaster!

Lan. My lord?

Gav. That Earl of Lancaster do I abhor. [*Aside.*

K. Edw. Will you not grant me this?—In spite of them
I'll have my will; and these two Mortimers,
That cross me thus, shall know I am displeased. [*Aside.*

E. Mor. If you love us, my lord, hate Gaveston.

Gav. That villain Mortimer! I'll be his death. [*Aside.*

Y. Mor. Mine uncle here, this earl, and I myself,
Were sworn to your father at his death,
That he should ne'er return into the realm:
And now, my lord, ere I will break my oath,
This sword of mine, that should offend your foes,
Shall sleep within the scabbard at thy need,
And underneath thy banners march who will,
For Mortimer will hang his armour up.

Gav. Mort dieu! [*Aside.*

K. Edw. Well, Mortimer, I'll make thee rue these words:
Beseems it thee to contradict thy king?
Frown'st thou thereat, aspiring Lancaster?
The sword shall plane the furrows of thy brows,
And hew these knees that now are grown so stiff.
I will have Gaveston; and you shall know
What danger 'tis to stand against your king.

Gav. Well done, Ned! [*Aside.*

Lan. My lord, why do you thus incense your peers,
That naturally would love and honour you,
But for that base and obscure Gaveston?
Four earldoms have I, besides Lancaster,—
Derby, Salisbury, Lincoln, Leicester;
These will I sell, to give my soldiers pay,
Ere Gaveston shall stay within the realm:
Therefore, if he be come, expel him straight.

Kent. Barons and earls, your pride hath made me mute;
But know I'll speak, and to the proof, I hope.
I do remember, in my father's days,
Lord Percy of the North, being highly mov'd,
Brav'd Mowbray in presence of the king;
For which, had not his highness lov'd him well,
He should have lost his head; but with his look

Th' undaunted spirit of Percy was appeas'd,
And Mowbray and he were reconcil'd:
Yet dare you brave the king unto his face.—
Brother, revenge it, and let these their heads
Preach upon poles, for trespass of their tongues.

War. O, our heads!

K. Edw. Ay, yours; and therefore I would wish you grant.

War. Bridle thy anger, gentle Mortimer.

Y. Mor. I cannot, nor I will not; I must speak.—
Cousin, our hands I hope shall fence our heads,
And strike off his that makes you threaten us.—
Come, uncle, let us leave the brain-sick king,
And henceforth parley with our naked swords.

E. Mor. Wiltshire hath men enough to save our heads.

War. All Warwickshire will leave him for my sake.

Lan. And northward Lancaster hath many friends.—
Adieu, my lord; and either change your mind,
Or look to see the throne, where you should sit,
To float in blood, and at thy wanton head
The glozing head of thy base minion thrown.
[*Exeunt all except King Edward, Kent, Gaveston,
and attendants.*

K. Edw. I cannot brook these haughty menaces:
Am I a king, and must be over-rul'd!—
Brother, display my ensigns in the field:
I'll bandy with the barons and the earls,
And either die or live with Gaveston.

Gav. I can no longer keep me from my lord. [*Comes forward.*

K. Edw. What, Gaveston! welcome! Kiss not my hand:
Embrace me, Gaveston, as I do thee.
Why shouldst thou kneel? know'st thou not who I am?
Thy friend, thyself, another Gaveston:
Not Hylas was more mourned for of Hercules
Than thou hast been of me since thy exile.

Gav. And, since I went from hence, no soul in hell
Hath felt more torment than poor Gaveston.

K. Edw. I know it.—Brother, welcome home my friend.—
Now let the treacherous Mortimers conspire,
And that high-minded Earl of Lancaster:
I have my wish, in that I joy thy sight;
And sooner shall the sea o'erwhelm my land
Than bear the ship that shall transport thee hence.

I here create thee Lord High-chamberlain,
Chief Secretary to the state and me,
Earl of Cornwall, King and Lord of Man.

Gav. My lord, these titles far exceed my worth.

Kent. Brother, the least of these may well suffice
For one of greater birth than Gaveston.

K. Edw. Cease, brother, for I cannot brook these words. —
Thy worth, sweet friend, is far above my gifts:
Therefore, to equal it, receive my heart.
If for these dignities thou be envied,
I'll give thee more; for, but to honour thee,
Is Edward pleas'd with kingly regiment.
Fear'st thou thy person? thou shalt have a guard:
Wantest thou gold? go to my treasury:
Wouldst thou be lov'd and fear'd? receive my seal,
Save or condemn, and in our name command
What so thy mind affects, or fancy likes.

Gav. It shall suffice me to enjoy your love;
Which whiles I have, I think myself as great
As Cæsar riding in the Roman street,
With captive kings at his triumphant car.

Enter the BISHOP OF COVENTRY.

K. Edw. Whither goes my Lord of Coventry so fast?

Bish. of Cov. To celebrate your father's exequies.
But is that wicked Gaveston return'd?

K. Edw. Ay, priest, and lives to be reveng'd on thee,
That wert the only cause of his exile.

Gav. 'Tis true; and, but for reverence of these robes,
Thou shouldst not plod one foot beyond this place.

Bish. of Cov. I did no more than I was bound to do:
And, Gaveston, unless thou be reclaim'd,
As then I did incense the parliament,
So will I now, and thou shalt back to France.

Gav. Saving your reverence, you must pardon me.

K. Edw. Throw off his golden mitre, rend his stole,
And in the channel christen him anew.

Kent. Ay, brother, lay not violent hands on him!
For he'll complain unto the see of Rome.

Gav. Let him complain unto the see of hell:
I'll be reveng'd on him for my exile.

K. Edw. No, spare his life, but seize upon his goods:

Be thou lord bishop, and receive his rents,
And make him serve thee as thy chaplain:
I give him thee; here, use him as thou wilt.

Gav. He shall to prison, and there die in bolts.

K. Edw. Ay, to the Tower, the Fleet, or where thou wilt.

Bish. of Cov. For this offence be thou accurs'd of God!

K. Edw. Who's there? Convey this priest to the Tower.

Bish. of Cov. True, true.

K. Edw. But, in the meantime, Gaveston, away,
And take possession of his house and goods.
Come, follow me, and thou shalt have my guard
To see it done, and bring thee safe again.

Gav. What should a priest do with so fair a house?
A prison may beseem his holiness.

[*Exeunt.*

SCENE II. LONDON, NEAR THE KING'S PAL-ACE

Enter, on one side, the elder MORTIMER, *and the younger*
MORTIMER; *on the other,* WARWICK, *and* LANCASTER.

War. 'Tis true, the bishop is in the Tower,
And goods and body given to Gaveston.

Lan. What, will they tyrannise upon the church?
Ah, wicked King! accursed Gaveston!
This ground, which is corrupted with their steps,
Shall be their timeless sepulchre or mine.

Y. Mor. Well, let that peevish Frenchman guard him sure;
Unless his breast be sword-proof, he shall die.

E. Mor. How now! why droops the Earl of Lancaster?

Y. Mor. Wherefore is Guy of Warwick discontent?

Lan. That villain Gaveston is made an earl.

E. Mor. An earl!

War. Ay, and besides Lord-chamberlain of the realm,
And Secretary too, and Lord of Man.

E. Mor. We may not nor we will not suffer this.

Y. Mor. Why post we not from hence to levy men?

Lan. "My Lord of Cornwall" now at every word;
And happy is the man whom he vouchsafes,
For vailing of his bonnet, one good look.
Thus, arm in arm, the king and he doth march:
Nay, more, the guard upon his lordship waits,
And all the court begins to flatter him.

War. Thus leaning on the shoulder of the king,
He nods, and scorns, and smiles at those that pass.

E. Mor. Doth no man take exceptions at the slave?

Lan. All stomach him, but none dare speak a word.

Y. Mor. Ah, that bewrays their baseness, Lancaster!
Were all the earls and barons of my mind,

We'd hale him from the bosom of the king,
And at the court-gate hang the peasant up,
Who, swoln with venom of ambitious pride,
Will be the ruin of the realm and us.

War. Here comes my Lord of Canterbury's grace.

Lan. His countenance bewrays he is displeas'd.

Enter the ARCHBISHOP OF CANTERBURY, *and an*
Attendant.

Archb. of Cant. First, were his sacred garments rent and torn;
Then laid they violent hands upon him; next,
Himself imprison'd, and his goods asseiz'd:
This certify the Pope: away, take horse. [*Exit Attendant.*

Lan. My lord, will you take arms against the king?

Archb. of Cant. What need I? God himself is up in arms
When violence is offer'd to the church.

Y. Mor. Then will you join with us, that be his peers,
To banish or behead that Gaveston?

Archb. of Cant. What else, my lords? for it concerns me near;
The bishoprick of Coventry is his.

Enter QUEEN ISABELLA.

Y. Mor. Madam, whither walks your majesty so fast?

Q. Isab. Unto the forest, gentle Mortimer,
To live in grief and baleful discontent;
For now my lord the king regards me not,
But dotes upon the love of Gaveston:
He claps his cheeks, and hangs about his neck,
Smiles in his face, and whispers in his ears;
And, when I come, he frowns, as who should say,
"Go whither thou wilt, seeing I have Gaveston."

E. Mor. Is it not strange that he is thus bewitch'd?

Y. Mor. Madam, return unto the court again:
That sly inveigling Frenchman we'll exile,
Or lose our lives; and yet, ere that day come,
The king shall lose his crown; for we have power,
And courage too, to be reveng'd at full.

Archb. of Cant. But yet lift not your swords against the king.

Lan. No; but we will lift Gaveston from hence.

War. And war must be the means, or he'll stay still.

Q. Isab. Then let him stay; for, rather than my lord
Shall be oppress'd with civil mutinies,

I will endure a melancholy life,
And let him frolic with his minion.

Archb. of Cant. My lords, to ease all this, but hear me speak:
We and the rest, that are his counsellors,
Will meet, and with a general consent
Confirm his banishment with our hands and seals.

Lan. What we confirm the king will frustrate.

Y. Mor. Then may we lawfully revolt from him.

War. But say, my lord, where shall this meeting be?

Archb. of Cant. At the New Temple.

Y. Mor. Content.

Archb. of Cant. And, in the meantime, I'll entreat you all
To cross to Lambeth, and there stay with me.

Lan. Come, then, let's away.

Y. Mor. Madam, farewell.

Q. Isab. Farewell, sweet Mortimer, and, for my sake,
Forbear to levy arms against the king.

Y. Mor. Ay, if words will serve; if not, I must.

[*Exeunt.*

SCENE III. LONDON, A STREET

Enter GAVESTON *and* KENT.

Gav. Edmund, the mighty prince of Lancaster,
That hath more earldoms than an ass can bear,
And both the Mortimers, two goodly men,
With Guy of Warwick, that redoubted knight,
Are gone towards Lambeth: there let them remain.

[*Exeunt.*

SCENE IV. LONDON, THE NEW TEMPLE.

Enter LANCASTER, WARWICK, PEMBROKE, *the elder*
MORTIMER, *the younger* MORTIMER, *the* ARCHBISHOP
OF CANTERBURY, *and* Attendants.

Lan. Here is the form of Gaveston's exile;
May it please your lordship to subscribe your name.

Archb. of Cant. Give me the paper.

[*He subscribes, as the others do after him.*

Lan. Quick, quick, my lord; I long to write my name.

War. But I long more to see him banish'd hence.

Y. Mor. The name of Mortimer shall fright the king,
Unless he be declin'd from that base peasant.

Enter KING EDWARD, GAVESTON, *and* KENT.

K. Edw. What, are you mov'd that Gaveston sits here?
It is our pleasure; we will have it so.

Lan. Your grace doth well to place him by your side,
For nowhere else the new earl is so safe.

E. Mor. What man of noble birth can brook this sight?
Quam male conveniunt! —
See, what a scornful look the peasant casts!

Pem. Can kingly lions fawn on creeping ants?

War. Ignoble vassal, that, like Phaeton,
Aspir'st unto the guidance of the sun!

Y. Mor. Their downfall is at hand, their forces down:
We will not thus be fac'd and over-peer'd.

K. Edw. Lay hands on that traitor Mortimer!

E. Mor. Lay hands on that traitor Gaveston!

Kent. Is this the duty that you owe your king?

War. We know our duties; let him know his peers.

K. Edw. Whither will you bear him? stay, or ye shall die.

E. Mor. We are no traitors; therefore threaten not.

Gav. No, threaten not, my lord, but pay them home.
Were I a king—

Y. Mor. Thou, villain! wherefore talk'st thou of a king,
That hardly art a gentleman by birth?

K. Edw. Were he a peasant, being my minion,
I'll make the proudest of you stoop to him.

Lan. My lord—you may not thus disparage us.—
Away, I say, with hateful Gaveston!

E. Mor. And with the Earl of Kent that favours him.
[*Attendants remove Gaveston and Kent.*

K. Edw. Nay, then, lay violent hands upon your king:
Here, Mortimer, sit thou in Edward's throne;
Warwick and Lancaster, wear you my crown.
Was ever king thus over-rul'd as I?

Lan. Learn, then, to rule us better, and the realm.

Y. Mor. What we have done, our heart-blood shall maintain.

War. Think you that we can brook this upstart['s] pride?

K. Edw. Anger and wrathful fury stops my speech.

Archb. of Cant. Why are you not mov'd? be patient, my lord,
And see what we your counsellors have done.

Y. Mor. My lords, now let us all be resolute,
And either have our wills, or lose our lives.

K. Edw. Meet you for this, proud over-daring peers!
Ere my sweet Gaveston shall part from me,
This isle shall fleet upon the ocean,
And wander to the unfrequented Inde.

Archb. of Cant. You know that I am legate to the Pope:
On your allegiance to the see of Rome,
Subscribe, as we have done, to his exile.

Y. Mor. Curse him, if he refuse; and then may we
Depose him, and elect another king.

K. Edw. Ay, there it goes! but yet I will not yield:
Curse me, depose me, do the worst you can.

Lan. Then linger not, my lord, but do it straight.

Archb. of Cant. Remember how the bishop was abus'd:
Either banish him that was the cause thereof,
Or I will presently discharge these lords
Of duty and allegiance due to thee.

K. Edw. It boots me not to threat; I must speak fair:
The legate of the Pope will be obey'd.— [*Aside.*

My lord, you shall be Chancellor of the realm;
Thou, Lancaster, High-Admiral of our fleet;
Young Mortimer and his uncle shall be earls;
And you, Lord Warwick, President of the North;
And thou of Wales. If this content you not,
Make several kingdoms of this monarchy,
And share it equally amongst you all,
So I may have some nook or corner left,
To frolic with my dearest Gaveston.

Archb. of Cant. Nothing shall alter us; we are resolv'd.

Lan. Come, come, subscribe.

Y. Mor. Why should you love him whom the world hates so?

K. Edw. Because he loves me more than all the world.
Ah, none but rude and savage-minded men
Would seek the ruin of my Gaveston!
You that be noble-born should pity him.

War. You that are princely-born should shake him off:
For shame, subscribe, and let the clown depart.

E. Mor. Urge him, my lord.

Archb. of Cant. Are you content to banish him the realm?

K. Edw. I see I must, and therefore am content:
Instead of ink, I'll write it with my tears. [*Subscribes.*

Y. Mor. The king is love-sick for his minion.

K. Edw. 'Tis done: and now, accursed hand, fall off!

Lan. Give it me: I'll have it publish'd in the streets.

Y. Mor. I'll see him presently despatch'd away.

Archb. of Cant. Now is my heart at ease.

War. And so is mine.

Pem. This will be good news to the common sort.

E. Mor. Be it or no, he shall not linger here.
[*Exeunt all except King Edward.*

K. Edw. How fast they run to banish him I love!
They would not stir, were it to do me good.
Why should a king be subject to a priest?
Proud Rome, that hatchest such imperial grooms,
With these thy superstitious taper-lights,
Wherewith thy antichristian churches blaze,
I'll fire thy crazed buildings, and enforce
The papal towers to kiss the lowly ground,
With slaughter'd priests make Tiber's channel swell,

And banks rais'd higher with their sepulchres!
As for the peers, that back the clergy thus,
If I be king, not one of them shall live.

Re-enter GAVESTON.

Gav. My lord, I hear it whisper'd everywhere,
That I am banish'd and must fly the land.

K. Edw. 'Tis true, sweet Gaveston: O were it false!
The legate of the Pope will have it so,
And thou must hence, or I shall be depos'd.
But I will reign to be reveng'd of them;
And therefore, sweet friend, take it patiently.
Live where thou wilt, I'll send thee gold enough;
And long thou shalt not stay; or, if thou dost,
I'll come to thee; my love shall ne'er decline.

Gav. Is all my hope turn'd to this hell of grief?

K. Edw. Rend not my heart with thy too-piercing words:
Thou from this land, I from myself am banish'd.

Gav. To go from hence grieves not poor Gaveston;
But to forsake you, in whose gracious looks
The blessedness of Gaveston remains;
For nowhere else seeks he felicity.

K. Edw. And only this torments my wretched soul,
That, whether I will or no, thou must depart.
Be governor of Ireland in my stead,
And there abide till fortune call thee home.
Here, take my picture, and let me wear thine:
[*They exchange pictures.*
O, might I keep thee here, as I do this,
Happy were I! but now most miserable.

Gav. 'Tis something to be pitied of a king.

K. Edw. Thou shalt not hence; I'll hide thee, Gaveston.

Gav. I shall be found, and then 'twill grieve me more.

K. Edw. Kind words and mutual talk makes our grief greater:
Therefore, with dumb embracement, let us part,
Stay, Gaveston; I cannot leave thee thus.

Gav. For every look, my love drops down a tear:
Seeing I must go, do not renew my sorrow.

K. Edw. The time is little that thou hast to stay,
And, therefore, give me leave to look my fill.
But, come, sweet friend; I'll bear thee on thy way.

Gav. The peers will frown.

K. Edw. I pass not for their anger. Come, let's go:
O, that we might as well return as go!

Enter QUEEN ISABELLA.

Q. Isab. Whither goes my lord?

K. Edw. Fawn not on me, French strumpet; get thee gone!

Q. Isab. On whom but on my husband should I fawn?

Gav. On Mortimer; with whom, ungentle queen,—
I judge no more—judge you the rest, my lord.

Q. Isab. In saying this, thou wrong'st me, Gaveston:
Is't not enough that thou corrupt'st my lord,
And art a bawd to his affections,
But thou must call mine honour thus in question?

Gav. I mean not so; your grace must pardon me.

K. Edw. Thou art too familiar with that Mortimer,
And by thy means is Gaveston exil'd:
But I would wish thee reconcile the lords,
Or thou shalt ne'er be reconcil'd to me.

Q. Isab. Your highness knows, it lies not in my power.

K. Edw. Away, then! touch me not.—Come, Gaveston.

Q. Isab. Villain, 'tis thou that robb'st me of my lord.

Gav. Madam, 'tis you that rob me of my lord.

K. Edw. Speak not unto her: let her droop and pine.

Q. Isab. Wherein, my lord, have I deserv'd these words?
Witness the tears that Isabella sheds,
Witness this heart, that, sighing for thee, breaks,
How dear my lord is to poor Isabel!

K. Edw. And witness heaven how dear thou art to me:
There weep; for, till my Gaveston be repeal'd,
Assure thyself thou com'st not in my sight.
[*Exeunt King Edward and Gaveston.*

Q. Isab. O miserable and distressed queen!
Would, when I left sweet France, and was embarked,
That charming Circe, walking on the waves,
Had chang'd my shape! or at the marriage-day
The cup of Hymen had been full of poison!
Or with those arms, that twin'd about my neck,
I had been stifled, and not liv'd to see
The king my lord thus to abandon me!
Like frantic Juno, will I fill the earth
With ghastly murmur of my sighs and cries;

For never doted Jove on Ganymede
So much as he on cursed Gaveston:
But that will more exasperate his wrath;
I must entreat him, I must speak him fair,
And be a means to call home Gaveston:
And yet he'll ever dote on Gaveston;
And so am I for ever miserable.

Re-enter LANCASTER, WARWICK, PEMBROKE, *the elder*
MORTIMER, *and the younger* MORTIMER.

Lan. Look, where the sister of the king of France
Sits wringing of her hands and beats her breast!

War. The king, I fear, hath ill-treated her.

Pem. Hard is the heart that injures such a saint.

Y. Mor. I know 'tis 'long of Gaveston she weeps.

E. Mor. Why, he is gone.

Y. Mor. Madam, how fares your grace?

Q. Isab. Ah, Mortimer, now breaks the king's hate forth,
And he confesseth that he loves me not!

Y. Mor. Cry quittance, madam, then, and love not him.

Q. Isab. No, rather will I die a thousand deaths:
And yet I love in vain; he'll ne'er love me.

Lan. Fear ye not, madam; now his minion's gone,
His wanton humour will be quickly left.

Q. Isab. O, never, Lancaster! I am enjoin'd,
To sue unto you all for his repeal:
This wills my lord, and this must I perform,
Or else be banish'd from his highness' presence.

Lan. For his repeal, madam! he comes not back,
Unless the sea cast up his shipwreck'd body.

War. And to behold so sweet a sight as that,
There's none here but would run his horse to death.

Y. Mor. But, madam, would you have us call him home?

Q. Isab. Ay, Mortimer, for, till he be restor'd,
The angry king hath banish'd me the court;
And, therefore, as thou lov'st and tender'st me,
Be thou my advocate unto these peers.

Y. Mor. What, would you have me plead for Gaveston?

E. Mor. Plead for him that will, I am resolv'd.

Lan. And so am I, my lord: dissuade the queen.

Q. Isab. O, Lancaster, let him dissuade the king!
For 'tis against my will he should return.

War. Then speak not for him; let the peasant go.

Q. Isab. 'Tis for myself I speak, and not for him.

Pem. No speaking will prevail; and therefore cease.

Y. Mor. Fair queen, forbear to angle for the fish
Which, being caught, strikes him that takes it dead;
I mean that vile torpedo, Gaveston,
That now, I hope, floats on the Irish seas.

Q. Isab. Sweet Mortimer, sit down by me a while,
And I will tell thee reasons of such weight
As thou wilt soon subscribe to his repeal.

Y. Mor. It is impossible: but speak your mind.

Q. Isab. Then, thus;—but none shall hear it but ourselves.
[*Talks to Y. Mor. apart.*

Lan. My lords, albeit the queen win Mortimer,
Will you be resolute and hold with me?

E. Mor. Not I, against my nephew.

Pem. Fear not; the queen's words cannot alter him.

War. No? do but mark how earnestly she pleads!

Lan. And see how coldly his looks make denial!

War. She smiles: now, for my life, his mind is chang'd!

Lan. I'll rather lose his friendship, I, than grant.

Y. Mor. Well, of necessity it must be so.—
My lords, that I abhor base Gaveston
I hope your honours make no question.
And therefore, though I plead for his repeal,
'Tis not for his sake, but to our avail;
Nay, for the realm's behoof, and for the king's.

Lan. Fie, Mortimer, dishonour not thyself!
Can this be true, 'twas good to banish him?
And is this true, to call him home again?
Such reasons make white black, and dark night day.

Y. Mor. My Lord of Lancaster, mark the respect.

Lan. In no respect can contraries be true.

Q. Isab. Yet, good my lord, hear what he can allege.

War. All that he speaks is nothing; we are resolv'd.

Y. Mor. Do you not wish that Gaveston were dead?

Pem. I would he were!

Y. Mor. Why, then, my lord, give me but leave to speak.

E. Mor. But, nephew, do not play the sophister.

Y. Mor. This which I urge is of a burning zeal
To mend the king and do our country good.
Know you not Gaveston hath store of gold,
Which may in Ireland purchase him such friends
As he will front the mightiest of us all?
And whereas he shall live and be belov'd,
'Tis hard for us to work his overthrow.

War. Mark you but that, my lord of Lancaster.

Y. Mor. But, were he here, detested as he is,
How easily might some base slave be suborn'd
To greet his lordship with a poniard,
And none so much as blame the murderer,
But rather praise him for that brave attempt,
And in the chronicle enrol his name
For purging of the realm of such a plague!

Pem. He saith true.

Lan. Ay, but how chance this was not done before?

Y. Mor. Because, my lords, it was not thought upon.
Nay, more, when he shall know it lies in us
To banish him, and then to call him home,
'Twill make him vail the top flag of his pride,
And fear to offend the meanest nobleman.

E. Mor. But how if he do not, nephew?

Y. Mor. Then may we with some colour rise in arms;
For, howsoever we have borne it out,
'Tis treason to be up against the king;
So shall we have the people of our side,
Which, for his father's sake, lean to the king,
But cannot brook a night-grown mushroom,
Such a one as my Lord of Cornwall is,
Should bear us down of the nobility:
And, when the commons and the nobles join,
'Tis not the king can buckler Gaveston;
We'll pull him from the strongest hold he hath.
My lords, if to perform this I be slack,
Think me as base a groom as Gaveston.

Lan. On that condition Lancaster will grant.

War. And so will Pembroke and I.

E. Mor. And I.

Y. Mor. In this I count me highly gratified,
And Mortimer will rest at your command.

Q. Isab. And when this favour Isabel forgets,
Then let her live abandon'd and forlorn.—
But see, in happy time, my lord the king,
Having brought the Earl of Cornwall on his way,
Is new return'd. This news will glad him much:
Yet not so much as me; I love him more
Than he can Gaveston: would he lov'd me
But half so much! then were I treble-blest.

Re-enter KING EDWARD, *mourning.*

K. Edw. He's gone, and for his absence thus I mourn:
Did never sorrow go so near my heart
As doth the want of my sweet Gaveston;
And, could my crown's revenue bring him back,
I would freely give it to his enemies,
And think I gain'd, having bought so dear a friend.

Q. Isab. Hark, how he harps upon his minion!

K. Edw. My heart is as an anvil unto sorrow,
Which beats upon it like the Cyclops' hammers,
And with the noise turns up my giddy brain,
And makes me frantic for my Gaveston.
Ah, had some bloodless Fury rose from hell,
And with my kingly sceptre struck me dead,
When I was forc'd to leave my Gaveston!

Lan. Diablo, what passions call you these?

Q. Isab. My gracious lord, I come to bring you news.

K. Edw. That you have parled with your Mortimer?

Q. Isab. That Gaveston, my lord, shall be repeal'd.

K. Edw. Repeal'd! the news is too sweet to be true.

Q. Isab. But will you love me, if you find it so?

K. Edw. If it be so, what will not Edward do?

Q. Isab. For Gaveston, but not for Isabel.

K. Edw. For thee, fair queen, if thou lov'st Gaveston;
I'll hang a golden tongue about thy neck,
Seeing thou hast pleaded with so good success.

Q. Isab. No other jewels hang about my neck
Than these, my lord; nor let me have more wealth
Than I may fetch from this rich treasury.

O, how a kiss revives poor Isabel!

K. Edw. Once more receive my hand; and let this be
A second marriage 'twixt thyself and me.

Q. Isab. And may it prove more happy than the first!
My gentle lord, bespeak these nobles fair,
That wait attendance for a gracious look,
And on their knees salute your majesty.

K. Edw. Courageous Lancaster, embrace thy king;
And, as gross vapours perish by the sun,
Even so let hatred with thy sovereign's smile:
Live thou with me as my companion.

Lan. This salutation overjoys my heart.

K. Edw. Warwick shall be my chiefest counsellor:
These silver hairs will more adorn my court
Than gaudy silks or rich embroidery.
Chide me, sweet Warwick, if I go astray.

War. Slay me, my lord, when I offend your grace.

K. Edw. In solemn triumphs and in public shows
Pembroke shall bear the sword before the king.

Pem. And with this sword Pembroke will fight for you.

K. Edw. But wherefore walks young Mortimer aside?
Be thou commander of our royal fleet;
Or, if that lofty office like thee not,
I make thee here Lord Marshal of the realm.

Y. Mor. My lord, I'll marshal so your enemies,
As England shall be quiet, and you safe.

K. Edw. And as for you, Lord Mortimer of Chirke,
Whose great achievements in our foreign war
Deserve no common place nor mean reward,
Be you the general of the levied troops
That now are ready to assail the Scots.

E. Mor. In this your grace hath highly honour'd me,
For with my nature war doth best agree.

Q. Isab. Now is the king of England rich and strong,
Having the love of his renowmed peers.

K. Edw. Ay, Isabel, ne'er was my heart so light.—
Clerk of the crown, direct our warrant forth,
For Gaveston, to Ireland!

Enter BEAUMONT *with warrant.*

Beaumont, fly

As fast as Iris or Jove's Mercury.

Beau. It shall be done, my gracious lord. [*Exit.*

K. Edw. Lord Mortimer, we leave you to your charge.
Now let us in, and feast it royally.
Against our friend the Earl of Cornwall comes
We'll have a general tilt and tournament;
And then his marriage shall be solemnis'd;
For wot you not that I have made him sure
Unto our cousin, the Earl of Glocester's heir?

Lan. Such news we hear, my lord.

K. Edw. That day, if not for him, yet for my sake,
Who in the triumph will be challenger,
Spare for no cost; we will requite your love.

War. In this or aught your highness shall command us.

K. Edw. Thanks, gentle Warwick. Come, lets in and revel.
[*Exeunt all except the elder Mortimer and the
younger Mortimer.*

E. Mor. Nephew, I must to Scotland; thou stay'st here.
Leave now to oppose thyself against the king:
Thou seest by nature he is mild and calm;
And, seeing his mind so dotes on Gaveston,
Let him without controlment have his will.
The mightiest kings have had their minions;
Great Alexander lov'd Hephæstion,
The conquering Hercules for Hylas wept,
And for Patroclus stern Achilles droop'd
And not kings only, but the wisest men;
The Roman Tully lov'd Octavius,
Grave Socrates wild Alcibiades.
Then let his grace, whose youth is flexible,
And promiseth as much as we can wish,
Freely enjoy that vain light-headed earl;
For riper years will wean him from such toys.

Y. Mor. Uncle, his wanton humour grieves not me;
But this I scorn, that one so basely-born
Should by his sovereign's favour grow so pert,
And riot it with the treasure of the realm,
While soldiers mutiny for want of pay.
He wears a lord's revenue on his back,
And, Midas-like, he jets it in the court,
With base outlandish cullions at his heels,
Whose proud fantastic liveries make such show
As if that Proteus, god of shapes, appear'd.

I have not seen a dapper Jack so brisk:
He wears a short Italian hooded cloak,
Larded with pearl, and in his Tuscan cap
A jewel of more value than the crown.
While others walk below, the king and he,
From out a window, laugh at such as we,
And flout our train, and jest at our attire.
Uncle, 'tis this that makes me impatient.

E. Mor. But, nephew, now you see the king is chang'd.

Y. Mor. Then so I am, and live to do him service:
But, whiles I have a sword, a hand, a heart,
I will not yield to any such upstart.
You know my mind: come, uncle, let's away.

[*Exeunt.*

ACT II.

SCENE I. A HALL IN THE EARL OF GLOCES-TER'S CASTLE.

Enter the younger SPENSER *and* BALDOCK.

Bald. Spenser,
Seeing that our lord the Earl of Glocester's dead,
Which of the nobles dost thou mean to serve?

Y. Spen. Not Mortimer, nor any of his side,
Because the king and he are enemies.
Baldock, learn this of me: a factious lord
Shall hardly do himself good, much less us;
But he that hath the favour of a king
May with one word advance us while we live.
The liberal Earl of Cornwall is the man
On whose good fortune Spenser's hope depends.

Bald. What, mean you, then, to be his follower?

Y. Spen. No, his companion; for he loves me well,
And would have once preferr'd me to the king.

Bald. But he is banish'd; there's small hope of him.

Y. Spen. Ay, for a while; but, Baldock, mark the end.
A friend of mine told me in secrecy
That he's repeal'd and sent for back again;
And even now a post came from the court
With letters to our lady from the king;
And, as she read, she smil'd; which makes me think
It is about her lover Gaveston.

Bald. 'Tis like enough; for, since he was exil'd,
She neither walks abroad nor comes in sight.
But I had thought the match had been broke off,
And that his banishment had chang'd her mind.

Y. Spen. Our lady's first love is not wavering;
My life for thine, she will have Gaveston.

Bald. Then hope I by her means to be preferr'd,
Having read unto her since she was a child.

Y. Spen. Then, Baldock, you must cast the scholar off,

And learn to court it like a gentleman.
'Tis not a black coat and a little band,
A velvet-cap'd cloak, fac'd before with serge,
And smelling to a nosegay all the day,
Or holding of a napkin in your hand,
Or saying a long grace at a table's end,
Or making low legs to a nobleman,
Or looking downward, with your eye-lids close,
And saying, "Truly, an't may please your honour,"
Can get you any favour with great men:
You must be proud, bold, pleasant, resolute,
And now and then stab, as occasion serves.

Bald. Spenser, thou know'st I hate such formal toys,
And use them but of mere hypocrisy.
Mine old lord, whiles he liv'd, was so precise,
That he would take exceptions at my buttons,
And, being like pins' heads, blame me for the bigness;
Which made me curate-like in mine attire,
Though inwardly licentious enough,
And apt for any kind of villany.
I am none of these common pedants, I,
That cannot speak without *propterea quod.*

Y. Spen. But one of those that saith *quando-quidem,*
And hath a special gift to form a verb.

Bald. Leave off this jesting; here my lady comes.

Enter KING EDWARD'S Niece.

Niece. The grief for his exile was not so much
As is the joy of his returning home.
This letter came from my sweet Gaveston:
What need'st thou, love, thus to excuse thyself?
I know thou couldst not come and visit me. [*Reads.*
I will not long be from thee, though I die; —
This argues the entire love of my lord; — [*Reads.*
When I forsake thee, death seize on my heart! —
But stay thee here where Gaveston shall sleep.
[*Puts the letter into her bosom.*
Now to the letter of my lord the king:
He wills me to repair unto the court,
And meet my Gaveston: why do I stay,
Seeing that he talks thus of my marriage day? —
Who's there? Baldock!
See that my coach be ready; I must hence.

Bald. It shall be done, madam.

Niece. And meet me at the park-pale presently [*Exit Baldock.*

Spenser, stay you, and bear me company,
For I have joyful news to tell thee of;
My lord of Cornwall is a-coming over,
And will be at the court as soon as we.

Y. Spen. I knew the king would have him home again.

Niece. If all things sort out, as I hope they will,
Thy service, Spenser, shall be thought upon.

Y. Spen. I humbly thank your ladyship.

Niece. Come, lead the way: I long till I am there.

[*Exeunt.*

SCENE II. TYNMOUTH CASTLE.

Enter KING EDWARD, QUEEN ISABELLA, KENT, LANCASTER, *the younger* MORTIMER, WARWICK, PEMBROKE, *and* Attendants.

K. Edw. The wind is good; I wonder why he stays:
I fear me he is wreck'd upon the sea.

Q. Isab. Look, Lancaster, how passionate he is,
And still his mind runs on his minion!

Lan. My lord,—

K. Edw. How now! what news? is Gaveston arriv'd?

Y. Mor. Nothing but Gaveston! what means your grace?
You have matters of more weight to think upon:
The King of France sets foot in Normandy.

K. Edw. A trifle! we'll expel him when we please.
But tell me, Mortimer, what's thy device
Against the stately triumph we decreed?

Y. Mor. A homely one, my lord, not worth the telling.

K. Edw. Pray thee, let me know it.

Y. Mor. But, seeing you are so desirous, thus it is;
A lofty cedar tree, fair flourishing,
On whose top branches kingly eagles perch,
And by the bark a canker creeps me up,
And gets unto the highest bough of all;
The motto, *Æque tandem.*

K. Edw. And what is yours, my Lord of Lancaster?

Lan. My lord, mine's more obscure than Mortimer's.
Pliny reports, there is a flying-fish
Which all the other fishes deadly hate,
And therefore, being pursu'd, it takes the air:
No sooner is it up, but there's a fowl
That seizeth it: this fish, my lord, I bear;
The motto this, *Undique mors est.*

Kent. Proud Mortimer! ungentle Lancaster!
Is this the love you bear your sovereign?

Is this the fruit your reconcilement bears?
Can you in words make show of amity,
And in your shields display your rancorous minds?
What call you this but private libelling
Against the Earl of Cornwall and my brother?

Q. Isab. Sweet husband, be content; they all love you.

K. Edw. They love me not that hate my Gaveston.
I am that cedar; shake me not too much;
And you the eagles; soar ye ne'er so high,
I have the jesses that will pull you down;
And *Æque tandem* shall that canker cry
Unto the proudest peer of Britainy.
Thou that compar'st him to a flying-fish,
And threaten'st death whether he rise or fall,
'Tis not the hugest monster of the sea,
Nor foulest harpy, that shall swallow him.

Y. Mor. If in his absence thus he favours him,
What will he do whenas he shall be present?

Lan. That shall we see: look, where his lordship come!

Enter GAVESTON.

K. Edw. My Gaveston! Welcome to Tynmouth! welcome to thy friend!
Thy absence made me droop and pine away;
For, as the lovers of fair Danaë,
When she was lock'd up in a brazen tower,
Desir'd her more, and wax'd outrageous,
So did it fare with me: and now thy sight
Is sweeter far than was thy parting hence
Bitter and irksome to my sobbing heart.

Gav. Sweet lord and king, your speech preventeth mine;
Yet have I words left to express my joy:
The shepherd, nipt with biting winter's rage,
Frolics not more to see the painted spring
Than I do to behold your majesty.

K. Edw. Will none of you salute my Gaveston?

Lan. Salute him! yes.—Welcome, Lord Chamberlain!

Y. Mor. Welcome is the good Earl of Cornwall!

War. Welcome, Lord Governor of the Isle of Man!

Pem. Welcome, Master Secretary!

Kent. Brother, do you hear them?

K. Edw. Still will these earls and barons use me thus?

Gav. My lord, I cannot brook these injuries.

Q. Isab. Ay me, poor soul, when these begin to jar!

[*Aside.*

K. Edw. Return it to their throats;
I'll be thy warrant.

Gav. Base, leaden earls, that glory in your birth,
Go sit at home, and eat your tenants' beef;
And come not here to scoff at Gaveston,
Whose mounting thoughts did never creep so low
As to bestow a look on such as you.

Lan. Yet I disdain not to do this for you.

[*Draws his sword, and offers to stab Gaveston.*

K. Edw. Treason! treason! where's the traitor?

Pem. Here, here!

K. Edw. Convey hence Gaveston; they'll murder him.

Gav. The life of thee shall salve this foul disgrace.

Y. Mor. Villain, thy life! unless I miss mine aim.

[*Wounds Gaveston.*

Q. Isab. Ah, furious Mortimer, what hast thou done.

Y. Mor. No more than I would answer, were he slain.

[*Exit Gaveston with Attendants.*

K. Edw. Yes, more than thou canst answer, though he live:
Dear shall you both abide this riotous deed:
Out of my presence! come not near the court.

Y. Mor. I'll not be barr'd the court for Gaveston.

Lan. We'll hale him by the ears unto the block.

K. Edw. Look to your own heads; his is sure enough.

War. Look to your own crown, if you back him thus.

Kent. Warwick, these words do ill beseem thy years.

K. Edw. Nay, all of them conspire to cross me thus:
But, if I live, I'll tread upon their heads
That think with high looks thus to tread me down.
Come, Edmund, let's away, and levy men:
'Tis war that must abate these barons' pride.

[*Exeunt King Edward, Queen Isabella, and Kent.*

War. Let's to our castles, for the king is mov'd.

Y. Mor. Mov'd may he be, and perish in his wrath!

Lan. Cousin, it is no dealing with him now;

He means to make us stoop by force of arms:
And therefore let us jointly here protest
To prosecute that Gaveston to the death.

Y. Mor. By heaven, the abject villain shall not live!

War. I'll have his blood, or die in seeking it.

Pem. The like oath Pembroke takes.

Lan. And so doth Lancaster.
Now send our heralds to defy the king;
And make the people swear to put him down.

Enter a Messenger.

Y. Mor. Letters! from whence?

Mes. From Scotland, my lord. [*Giving letters to Mortimer.*

Lan. Why, how now, cousin! how fare all our friends?

Y. Mor. My uncle's taken prisoner by the Scots.

Lan. We'll have him ransom'd, man: be of good cheer.

Y. Mor. They rate his ransom at five thousand pound.
Who should defray the money but the king,
Seeing he is taken prisoner in his wars?
I'll to the king.

Lan. Do, cousin, and I'll bear thee company.

War. Meantime my Lord of Pembroke and myself
Will to Newcastle here, and gather head.

Y. Mor. About it, then, and we will follow you.

Lan. Be resolute and full of secrecy.

War. I warrant you.

[*Exit with Pembroke.*

Y. Mor. Cousin, an if he will not ransom him,
I'll thunder such a peal into his ears
As never subject did unto his king.

Lan. Content; I'll bear my part.—Hollo! who's there?

Enter Guard.

Y. Mor. Ay, marry, such a guard as this doth well.

Lan. Lead on the way.

Guard. Whither will your lordships?

Y. Mor. Whither else but to the king?

Guard. His highness is dispos'd to be alone.

Lan. Why, so he may; but we will speak to him.

Guard. You may not in, my lord.

Y. Mor. May we not?

Enter KING EDWARD *and* KENT.

K. Edw. How now!
What noise is this? who have we here? is't you? [*Going.*

Y. Mor. Nay, stay, my lord; I come to bring you news;
Mine uncle's taken prisoner by the Scots.

K. Edw. Then ransom him.

Lan. 'Twas in your wars; you should ransom him.

Y. Mor. And you will ransom him, or else—

Kent. What, Mortimer, you will not threaten him?

K. Edw. Quiet yourself; you shall have the broad seal,
To gather for him th[o]roughout the realm.

Lan. Your minion Gaveston hath taught you this.

Y. Mor. My lord, the family of the Mortimers
Are not so poor, but, would they sell their land,
'Twould levy men enough to anger you.
We never beg, but use such prayers as these.

K. Edw. Shall I still be haunted thus?

Y. Mor. Nay, now you are here alone, I'll speak my mind.

Lan. And so will I; and then, my lord, farewell.

Y. Mor. The idle triumphs, masks, lascivious shows,
And prodigal gifts bestow'd on Gaveston,
Have drawn thy treasury dry, and made thee weak;
The murmuring commons, overstretched, break.

Lan. Look for rebellion, look to be depos'd:
Thy garrisons are beaten out of France,
And, lame and poor, lie groaning at the gates;
The wild Oneil, with swarms of Irish kerns,
Lives uncontroll'd within the English pale;
Unto the walls of York the Scots make road,
And, unresisted, drive away rich spoils.

Y. Mor. The haughty Dane commands the narrow seas,
While in the harbour ride thy ships unrigg'd.

Lan. What foreign prince sends thee ambassadors?

Y. Mor. Who loves thee, but a sort of flatterers?

Lan. Thy gentle queen, sole sister to Valois,
Complains that thou hast left her all forlorn.

Y. Mor. Thy court is naked, being bereft of those

That make a king seem glorious to the world,
I mean the peers, whom thou shouldst dearly love;
Libels are cast against thee in the street;
Ballads and rhymes made of thy overthrow.

Lan. The northern borderers, seeing their houses burnt,
Their wives and children slain, run up and down,
Cursing the name of thee and Gaveston.

Y. Mor. When wert thou in the field with banner spread,
But once? and then thy soldiers march'd like players,
With garish robes, not armour; and thyself,
Bedaub'd with gold, rode laughing at the rest,
Nodding and shaking of thy spangled crest,
Where women's favours hung like labels down.

Lan. And thereof came it that the fleering Scots,
To England's high disgrace, have made this jig;
Maids of England, sore may you mourn,
For your lemans you have lost at Bannocksbourn, —
With a heave and a ho!
What weeneth the king of England
So soon to have won Scotland! —
With a rombelow!

Y. Mor. Wigmore shall fly, to set my uncle free.

Lan. And, when 'tis gone, our swords shall purchase more.
If you be mov'd, revenge it as you can:
Look next to see us with our ensigns spread. [*Exit with Y. Mortimer.*

K. Edw. My swelling heart for very anger breaks:
How oft have I been baited by these peers,
And dare not be reveng'd, for their power is great!
Yet, shall the crowning of these cockerels
Affright a lion? Edward, unfold thy paws,
And let their lives'-blood slake thy fury's hunger.
If I be cruel and grow tyrannous,
Now let them thank themselves, and rue too late.

Kent. My lord, I see your love to Gaveston
Will be the ruin of the realm and you,
For now the wrathful nobles threaten wars;
And therefore, brother, banish him for ever.

K. Edw. Art thou an enemy to my Gaveston?

Kent. Ay; and it grieves me that I favour'd him.

K. Edw. Traitor, be gone! whine thou with Mortimer.

Kent. So will I, rather than with Gaveston.

K. Edw. Out of my sight, and trouble me no more!

Kent. No marvel though thou scorn thy noble peers,
When I thy brother am rejected thus.

K. Edw. Away! [*Exit Kent.*
Poor Gaveston, thou hast no friend but me!
Do what they can, we'll live in Tynmouth here;
And, so I walk with him about the walls,
What care I though the earls begirt us round?
Here comes she that is cause of all these jars.

Enter QUEEN ISABELLA, *with* EDWARD'S NIECE, *two* Ladies,
GAVESTON, BALDOCK, *and the younger* SPENSER.

Q. Isab. My lord, 'tis thought the earls are up in arms.

K. Edw. Ay, and 'tis likewise thought you favour 'em.

Q. Isab. Thus do you still suspect me without cause.

Niece. Sweet uncle, speak more kindly to the queen.

Gav. My lord, dissemble with her; speak her fair.

K. Edw. Pardon me, sweet; I forgot myself.

Q. Isab. Your pardon is quickly got of Isabel.

K. Edw. The younger Mortimer is grown so brave,
That to my face he threatens civil wars.

Gav. Why do you not commit him to the Tower?

K. Edw. I dare not, for the people love him well.

Gav. Why, then, we'll have him privily made away.

K. Edw. Would Lancaster and he had both carous'd
A bowl of poison to each other's health!
But let them go, and tell me what are these.

Niece. Two of my father's servants whilst he liv'd:
May't please your grace to entertain them now.

K. Edw. Tell me, where wast thou born? what is thine arms?

Bald. My name is Baldock, and my gentry
I fetch from Oxford, not from heraldry.

K. Edw. The fitter art thou, Baldock, for my turn.
Wait on me, and I'll see thou shalt not want.

Bald. I humbly thank your majesty.

K. Edw. Knowest thou him, Gaveston.

Gav. Ay, my lord; His name is Spenser; he is well allied:
For my sake let him wait upon your grace;
Scarce shall you find a man of more desert.

K. Edw. Then, Spenser, wait upon me for his sake:

L I'll grace thee with a higher style ere long.

Y. Spen. No greater titles happen unto me
Than to be favour'd of your majesty!

K. Edw. Cousin, this day shall be your marriage feast:—
And, Gaveston, think that I love thee well,
To wed thee to our niece, the only heir
Unto the Earl of Glocester late deceas'd.

Gav. I know, my lord, many will stomach me;
But I respect neither their love nor hate.

K. Edw. The headstrong barons shall not limit me;
He that I list to favour shall be great.
Come, let's away; and, when the marriage ends,
Have at the rebels and their complices!

[*Exeunt.*

SCENE III. THE BARON'S CAMP BEFORE

Enter KENT, LANCASTER, *the younger* MORTIMER,
WARWICK, PEMBROKE, *and others.*

Kent. My lords, of love to this our native land,
I come to join with you, and leave the king;
And in your quarrel, and the realm's behoof,
Will be the first that shall adventure life.

Lan. I fear me, you are sent of policy,
To undermine us with a show of love.

War. He is your brother; therefore have we cause
To cast the worst, and doubt of your revolt.

Kent. Mine honour shall be hostage of my truth:
If that will not suffice, farewell, my lords.

Y. Mor. Stay, Edmund: never was Plantagenet
False of his word; and therefore trust we thee.

Pem. But what's the reason you should leave him now?

Kent. I have inform'd the Earl of Lancaster.

Lan. And it sufficeth. Now, my lords, know this,
That Gaveston is secretly arriv'd,
And here in Tynmouth frolics with the king.
Let us with these our followers scale the walls,
And suddenly surprise them unawares.

Y. Mor. I'll give the onset.

War. And I'll follow thee.

Y. Mor. This tatter'd ensign of my ancestors,
Which swept the desert shore of that Dead Sea
Whereof we got the name of Mortimer,
Will I advance upon this castle ['s] walls—
Drums, strike alarum, raise them from their sport,
And ring aloud the knell of Gaveston!

Lan. None be so hardy as to touch the king;
But neither spare you Gaveston nor his friends. [*Exeunt.*

SCENE IV. WITHIN TYNMOUTH CASTLE.

Enter, severally KING EDWARD *and the younger* SPENSER.

K. Edw. O, tell me, Spenser, where is Gaveston?

Y. Spen. I fear me he is slain, my gracious lord.

K. Edw. No, here he comes; now let them spoil and kill.

Enter QUEEN ISABELLA, KING EDWARD'S Niece, GAVESTON, *and* Nobles.

Fly, fly, my lords; the earls have got the hold;
Take shipping, and away to Scarborough:
Spenser and I will post away by land.

Gav. O, stay, my lord! they will not injure you.

K. Edw. I will not trust them. Gaveston, away!

Gav. Farewell, my lord.

K. Edw. Lady, farewell.

Niece. Farewell, sweet uncle, till we meet again.

K. Edw. Farewell, sweet Gaveston; and farewell, niece.

Q. Isab. No farewell to poor Isabel thy queen?

K. Edw. Yes, yes, for Mortimer your lover's sake.

Q. Isab. Heavens can witness, I love none but you.
[*Exeunt all except Queen Isabella.*
From my embracements thus he breaks away.
O, that mine arms could close this isle about,
That I might pull him to me where I would!
Or that these tears, that drizzle from mine eyes,
Had power to mollify his stony heart,
That, when I had him, we might never part!

Enter LANCASTER, WARWICK, *the younger* MORTIMER, *and*

others. Alarums within.

Lan. I wonder how he scap'd.

Y. Mor. Who's this? the queen!

Q. Isab. Ay, Mortimer, the miserable queen,

Whose pining heart her inward sighs have blasted,
And body with continual mourning wasted:
These hands are tir'd with haling of my lord
From Gaveston, from wicked Gaveston;
And all in vain; for, when I speak him fair,
He turns away, and smiles upon his minion.

Y. Mor. Cease to lament, and tell us where's the king?

Q. Isab. What would you with the king? is't him you seek?

Lan. No, madam, but that cursed Gaveston:
Far be it from the thought of Lancaster
To offer violence to his sovereign!
We would but rid the realm of Gaveston:
Tell us where he remains, and he shall die.

Q. Isab. He's gone by water unto Scarborough:
Pursue him quickly, and he cannot scape;
The king hath left him, and his train is small.

War. Forslow no time, sweet Lancaster; let's march.

Y. Mor. How comes it that the king and he is parted?

Q. Isab. That thus your army, going several ways,
Might be of lesser force, and with the power
That he intendeth presently to raise,
Be easily suppress'd: therefore be gone.

Y. Mor. Here in the river rides a Flemish hoy:
Let's all aboard, and follow him amain.

Lan. The wind that bears him hence will fill our sails;
Come, come, aboard! 'tis but an hour's sailing.

Y. Mor. Madam, stay you within this castle here.

Q. Isab. No, Mortimer; I'll to my lord the king.

Y. Mor. Nay, rather sail with us to Scarborough.

Q. Isab. You know the king is so suspicious
As, if he hear I have but talk'd with you,
Mine honour will be call'd in question;
And therefore, gentle Mortimer, be gone.

Y. Mor. Madam, I cannot stay to answer you:
But think of Mortimer as he deserves.

[*Exeunt all except Queen Isabella.*

Q. Isab. So well hast thou deserv'd, sweet Mortimer,
As Isabel could live with thee for ever.
In vain I look for love at Edward's hand,
Whose eyes are fix'd on none but Gaveston.

Yet once more I'll importune him with prayer:
If he be strange, and not regard my words,
My son and I will over into France,
And to the king my brother there complain
How Gaveston hath robb'd me of his love:
But yet, I hope, my sorrows will have end,
And Gaveston this blessed day be slain.

[*Exit.*

SCENE V. COUNTRY NEAR SCARBOROUGH CASTLE

Enter GAVESTON, *pursued.*

Gav. Yet, lusty lords, I have escap'd your hands,
Your threats, your 'larums, and your hot pursuits;
And, though divorced from King Edward's eyes,
Yet liveth Pierce of Gaveston unsurpris'd,
Breathing in hope (malgrado all your beards,
That muster rebels thus against your king)
To see his royal sovereign once again.

Enter WARWICK, LANCASTER, PEMBROKE, *the younger*
MORTIMER, Soldiers, JAMES *and other* Attendants *of*
PENBROKE.

War. Upon him, soldiers! take away his weapons!

Y. Mor. Thou proud disturber of thy country's peace,
Corrupter of thy king, cause of these broils,
Base flatterer, yield! and, were it not for shame,
Shame and dishonour to a soldier's name,
Upon my weapon's point here shouldst thou fall,
And welter in thy gore.

Lan. Monster of men,
That, like the Greekish strumpet, train'd to arms
And bloody wars so many valiant knights,
Look for no other fortune, wretch, than death!
King Edward is not here to buckler thee.

War. Lancaster, why talk'st thou to the slave?—
Go, soldiers, take him hence; for, by my sword,
His head shall off.—Gaveston, short warning
Shall serve thy turn: it is our country's cause
That here severely we will execute
Upon thy person.—Hang him at a bough.

Gav. My lord,—

War. Soldiers, have him away.—
But, for thou wert the favourite of a king,
Thou shalt have so much honour at our hands.

Gav. I thank you all, my lords: then I perceive
That heading is one, and hanging is the other,
And death is all.

Enter ARUNDEL.

Lan. How now, my Lord of Arundel!

Arun. My lords, King Edward greets you all by me.

War. Arundel, say your message.

Arun. His majesty, hearing that you had taken Gaveston,
Entreateth you by me, yet but he may
See him before he dies; for why, he says,
And sends you word, he knows that die he shall;
And, if you gratify his grace so far,
He will be mindful of the courtesy.

War. How now!

Gav. Renowmed Edward, how thy name
Revives poor Gaveston!

War. No, it needeth not:
Arundel, we will gratify the king
In other matters; he must pardon us in this.—
Soldiers, away with him!

Gav. Why, my Lord of Warwick,
Will now these short delays beget my hopes?
I know it, lords, it is life you aim at,
Yet grant King Edward this.

Y. Mor. Shalt thou appoint
What we shall grant?—Soldiers, away with him!—
Thus we'll gratify the king;
We'll send his head by thee; let him bestow
His tears on that, for that is all he gets
Of Gaveston, or else his senseless trunk.

Lan. Not so, my lord, lest he bestow more cost
In burying him than he hath ever earn'd.

Arun. My lords, it is his majesty's request,
And in the honour of a king he swears,
He will but talk with him, and send him back.

War. When, can you tell? Arundel, no; we wot
He that the care of his realm remits,
And drives his nobles to these exigents
For Gaveston, will, if he seize him once,
Violate any promise to possess him.

Arun. Then, if you will not trust his grace in keep,

My lords, I will be pledge for his return.

Y. Mor. 'Tis honourable in thee to offer this;
But, for we know thou art a noble gentleman,
We will not wrong thee so,
To make away a true man for a thief.

Gav. How mean'st thou, Mortimer? that is over-base.

Y. Mor. Away, base groom, robber of king's renown!
Question with thy companions and mates.

Pem. My Lord Mortimer, and you, my lords, each one,
To gratify the king's request therein,
Touching the sending of this Gaveston,
Because his majesty so earnestly
Desires to see the man before his death,
I will upon mine honour undertake
To carry him, and bring him back again;
Provided this, that you, my Lord of Arundel,
Will join with me.

War. Pembroke, what wilt thou do?
Cause yet more bloodshed? is it not enough
That we have taken him, but must we now
Leave him on "Had I wist," and let him go?

Pem. My lords, I will not over-woo your honours:
But, if you dare trust Pembroke with the prisoner,
Upon mine oath, I will return him back.

Arun. My Lord of Lancaster, what say you in this?

Lan. Why, I say, let him go on Pembroke's word.

Pem. And you, Lord Mortimer?

Y. Mor. How say you, my Lord of Warwick?

War. Nay, do your pleasures: I know how 'twill prove.

Pem. Then give him me.

Gav. Sweet sovereign, yet I come
To see thee ere I die!

War. Yet not perhaps,
If Warwick's wit and policy prevail. [*Aside.*

Y. Mor. My Lord of Pembroke, we deliver him you:
Return him on your honour.—Sound, away!
[*Exeunt all except Pembroke, Arundel, Gaveston, James
and other attendants of Pembroke.*

Pem. My lord, you shall go with me:
My house is not far hence; out of the way

A little; but our men shall go along.
We that have pretty wenches to our wives,
Sir, must not come so near to balk their lips.

Arun. 'Tis very kindly spoke, my Lord of Pembroke:
Your honour hath an adamant of power
To draw a prince.

Pem. So, my lord.—Come hither, James:
I do commit this Gaveston to thee;
Be thou this night his keeper; in the morning
We will discharge thee of thy charge: be gone.

Gav. Unhappy Gaveston, whither go'st thou now?
[*Exit with James and other Attendants of Pembroke.*

Horse-boy. My lord, we'll quickly be at Cobham.

[*Exeunt.*

ACT III.

SCENE I. COUNTRY NEAR DEDDINGTON.

Enter GAVESTON *mourning,* JAMES *and other* Attendants *of* PEMBROKE.

Gav. O treacherous Warwick, thus to wrong thy friend!

James. I see it is your life these arms pursue.

Gav. Weaponless must I fall, and die in bands?
O, must this day be period of my life,
Centre of all my bliss? And ye be men,
Speed to the king.

Enter WARWICK *and* Soldiers.

War. My Lord of Pembroke's men,
Strive you no longer: I will have that Gaveston.

James. Your lordship doth dishonour to yourself,
And wrong our lord, your honourable friend.

War. No, James, it is my country's cause I follow. —
Go, take the villain: soldiers, come away;
We'll make quick work. — Commend me to your master,
My friend, and tell him that I watch'd it well. —
Come, let thy shadow parley with King Edward.

Gav. Treacherous earl, shall I not see the king?

War. The king of heaven perhaps, no other king. —
Away! [*Exeunt Warwick and Soldiers with Gaveston.*

James. Come, fellows: it booted not for us to strive:
We will in haste go certify our lord.

[*Exeunt.*

SCENE II. KING'S CAMP, NEAR BOROUGH-BRIDGE, YORKSHIRE.

Enter KING EDWARD, *the younger* SPENSER, BALDOCK, Noblemen
of the king's side, and Soldiers *with drums and fifes.*

K. Edw. I long to hear an answer from the barons
Touching my friend, my dearest Gaveston.
Ah, Spenser, not the riches of my realm
Can ransom him! ah, he is mark'd to die!
I know the malice of the younger Mortimer;
Warwick I know is rough, and Lancaster
Inexorable; and I shall never see
My lovely Pierce of Gaveston again:
The barons overbear with me their pride.

Y. Spen. Were I King Edward, England's sovereign,
Son to the lovely Eleanor of Spain,
Great Edward Longshanks' issue, would I bear
These braves, this rage, and suffer uncontroll'd
These barons thus to beard me in my land,
In mine own realm? My lord, pardon my speech:
Did you retain your father's magnanimity,
Did you regard the honour of your name,
You would not suffer thus your majesty
Be counterbuff'd of your nobility.
Strike off their heads, and let them preach on poles:
No doubt, such lessons they will teach the rest,
As by their preachments they will profit much,
And learn obedience to their lawful king.

K. Edw. Yes, gentle Spenser, we have been too mild,
Too kind to them; but now have drawn our sword,
And, if they send me not my Gaveston,
We'll steel it on their crest[s], and poll their tops.

Bald. This haught resolve becomes your majesty,
Not to be tied to their affection,
As though your highness were a school-boy still,
And must be aw'd and govern'd like a child.

Enter the elder SPENSER *with his truncheon, and*

Soldiers.

E. Spen. Long live my sovereign, the noble Edward,
In peace triumphant, fortunate in wars!

K. Edw. Welcome, old man: com'st thou in Edward's aid?
Then tell thy prince of whence and what thou art.

E. Spen. Low, with a band of bow-men and of pikes,
Brown bills and targeteers, four hundred strong,
Sworn to defend King Edward's royal right,
I come in person to your majesty,
Spenser, the father of Hugh Spenser there,
Bound to your highness everlastingly
For favour done, in him, unto us all.

K. Edw. Thy father, Spenser?

Y. Spen. True, an it like your grace,
That pours, in lieu of all your goodness shown,
His life, my lord, before your princely feet.

K. Edw. Welcome ten thousand times, old man, again!
Spenser, this love, this kindness to thy king,
Argues thy noble mind and disposition.
Spenser, I here create thee Earl of Wiltshire,
And daily will enrich thee with our favour,
That, as the sunshine, shall reflect o'er thee.
Beside, the more to manifest our love,
Because we hear Lord Bruce doth sell his land,
And that the Mortimers are in hand withal,
Thou shalt have crowns of us t'outbid the barons;
And, Spenser, spare them not, lay it on.—
Soldiers, a largess, and thrice-welcome all!

Y. Spen. My lord, here comes the queen.

Enter QUEEN ISABELLA, PRINCE EDWARD, *and*
LEVUNE.

K. Edw. Madam, what news?

Q. Isab. News of dishonour, lord, and discontent.
Our friend Levune, faithful and full of trust,
Informeth us, by letters and by words,
That Lord Valois our brother, King of France,
Because your highness hath been slack in homage,
Hath seized Normandy into his hands:
These be the letters, this the messenger.

K. Edw. Welcome, Levune.—Tush, Sib, if this be all,
Valois and I will soon be friends again.—
But to my Gaveston: shall I never see,

Never behold thee now!—Madam, in this matter
We will employ you and your little son;
You shall go parley with the King of France.—
Boy, see you bear you bravely to the king,
And do your message with a majesty.

P. Edw. Commit not to my youth things of more weight
Than fits a prince so young as I to bear;
And fear not, lord and father,—heaven's great beams
On Atlas' shoulder shall not lie more safe
Than shall your charge committed to my trust.

Q. Isab. Ah, boy, this towardness makes thy mother fear
Thou art not mark'd to many days on earth!

K. Edw. Madam, we will that you with speed be shipp'd,
And this our son; Levune shall follow you
With all the haste we can despatch him hence.
Choose of our lords to bear you company;
And go in peace; leave us in wars at home.

Q. Isab. Unnatural wars, where subjects brave their king:
God end them once!—My lord, I take my leave,
To make my preparation for France. [*Exit with Prince Edward.*

Enter ARUNDEL.

K. Edw. What, Lord Arundel, dost thou come alone?

Arun. Yea, my good lord, for Gaveston is dead.

K. Edw. Ah, traitors, have they put my friend to death?
Tell me, Arundel, died he ere thou cam'st,
Or didst thou see my friend to take his death?

Arun. Neither, my lord; for, as he was surpris'd,
Begirt with weapons and with enemies round,
I did your highness' message to them all,
Demanding him of them, entreating rather,
And said, upon the honour of my name,
That I would undertake to carry him
Unto your highness, and to bring him back.

K. Edw. And, tell me, would the rebels deny me that?

Y. Spen. Proud recreants!

K. Edw. Yea, Spenser, traitors all!

Arun. In found them at the first inexorable;
The Earl of Warwick would not bide the hearing,
Mortimer hardly; Pembroke and Lancaster
Spake least; and when they flatly had denied,
Refusing to receive me pledge for him,

The Earl of Pembroke mildly thus bespake;
"My lord, because our sovereign sends for him,
And promiseth he shall be safe return'd,
I will this undertake, to have him hence,
And see him re-deliver'd to your hands."

K. Edw. Well, and how fortunes [it] that he came not?

Y. Spen. Some treason or some villany was cause.

Arun. The Earl of Warwick seiz'd him on his way;
For, being deliver'd unto Pembroke's men,
Their lord rode home, thinking his prisoner safe;
But, ere he came, Warwick in ambush lay,
And bare him to his death; and in a trench
Strake off his head, and march'd unto the camp.

Y. Spen. A bloody part, flatly 'gainst law of arms!

K. Edw. O, shall I speak, or shall I sigh and die!

Y. Spen. My lord, refer your vengeance to the sword
Upon these barons; hearten up your men;
Let them not unreveng'd murder your friends:
Advance your standard, Edward, in the field,
And march to fire them from their starting-holes.

K. Edw. [*kneeling.*] By earth, the common mother of us all,
By heaven, and all the moving orbs thereof,
By this right hand, and by my father's sword,
And all the honours 'longing to my crown,
I will have heads and lives for him as many
As I have manors, castles, towns, and towers!— [*Rises.*
Treacherous Warwick! traitorous Mortimer!
If I be England's king, in lakes of gore
Your headless trunks, your bodies will I trail,
That you may drink your fill, and quaff in blood,
And stain my royal standard with the same,
That so my bloody colours may suggest
Remembrance of revenge immortally
On your accursed traitorous progeny,
You villains that have slain my Gaveston!—
And in this place of honour and of trust,
Spenser, sweet Spenser, I adopt thee here;
And merely of our love we do create thee
Earl of Glocester and Lord Chamberlain,
Despite of times, despite of enemies.

Y. Spen. My lord, here's a messenger from the barons
Desires access unto your majesty.

K. Edw. Admit him near.

Enter Herald *with his coat of arms.*

Her. Long live King Edward, England's lawful lord!

K. Edw. So wish not they, I wis, that sent thee hither:
Thou com'st from Mortimer and his complices:
A ranker rout of rebels never was.
Well, say thy message.

Her. The barons, up in arms, by me salute
Your highness with long life and happiness;
And bid me say, as plainer to your grace,
That if without effusion of blood
You will this grief have ease and remedy,
That from your princely person you remove
This Spenser, as a putrifying branch
That deads the royal vine, whose golden leaves
Empale your princely head, your diadem;
Whose brightness such pernicious upstarts dim,
Say they, and lovingly advise your grace
To cherish virtue and nobility,
And have old servitors in high esteem,
And shake off smooth dissembling flatterers:
This granted, they, their honours, and their lives,
Are to your highness vow'd and consecrate.

Y. Spen. Ah, traitors, will they still display their pride?

K. Edw. Away! tarry no answer, but be gone! —
Rebels, will they appoint their sovereign
His sports, his pleasures, and his company? —
Yet, ere thou go, see how I do divorce [*Embraces young Spenser.*
Spenser from thee. Now get thee to thy lords,
And tell them I will come to chastise them
For murdering Gaveston: hie thee, get thee gone!
Edward, with fire and sword, follows at thy heels. [*Exit Herald.*
My lord[s], perceive you how these rebels swell? —
Soldiers, good hearts! defend your sovereign's right,
For, now, even now, we march to make them stoop.
Away!

[*Exeunt. Alarums, excursions, a great fight, and a
retreat sounded, within.*

SCENE III. ANOTHER PART OF THE FIELD, BOROUGHBRIDGE.

Re-enter KING EDWARD, *the elder* SPENSER, *the younger* SPENSER, BALDOCK, *and* Noblemen *of the king's side.*

K. Edw. Why do we sound retreat? upon them, lords!
This day I shall your vengeance with my sword
On those proud rebels that are up in arms,
And do confront and countermand their king.

Y. Spen. I doubt it not, my lord; right will prevail.

E. Spen. 'Tis not amiss, my liege, for either part
To breathe a while; our men, with sweat and dust
All chok'd well near, begin to faint for heat;
And this retire refresheth horse and man.

Y. Spen. Here come the rebels.

Enter the younger MORTIMER, LANCASTER, WARWICK, PEMBROKE, *and others.*

Y. Mor. Look, Lancaster, yonder is Edward Among his flatterers.

Lan. And there let him be,
Till he pay dearly for their company.

War. And shall, or Warwick's sword shall smite in vain.

K. Edw. What, rebels, do you shrink and sound retreat?

Y. Mor. No, Edward, no; thy flatterers faint and fly.

Lan. They'd best betimes forsake thee and their trains,
For they'll betray thee, traitors as they are.

Y. Spen. Traitor on thy face, rebellious Lancaster!

Pem. Away, base upstart! brav'st thou nobles thus?

E. Spen. A noble attempt and honourable deed,
Is it not, trow ye, to assemble aid
And levy arms against your lawful king?

K. Edw. For which, ere long, their heads shall satisfy
T' appease the wrath of their offended king.

Y. Mor. Then, Edward, thou wilt fight it to the last,

And rather bathe thy sword in subjects' blood
Than banish that pernicious company?

K. Edw. Ay, traitors all, rather than thus be brav'd,
Make England's civil towns huge heaps of stones,
And ploughs to go about our palace-gates.

War. A desperate and unnatural resolution! —
Alarum to the fight!
Saint George for England, and the barons' right!

K. Edw. Saint George for England, and King Edward's right!

[*Alarums. Exeunt the two parties severally.*

Enter KING EDWARD *and his followers, with the* Barons *and* KENT *captive.*

K. Edw. Now, lusty lords, now not by chance of war,
But justice of the quarrel and the cause,
Vail'd is your pride: methinks you hang the heads
But we'll advance them, traitors: now 'tis time
To be aveng'd on you for all your braves,
And for the murder of my dearest friend,
To whom right well you knew our soul was knit,
Good Pierce of Gaveston, my sweet favourite:
Ah, rebels, recreants, you made him away!

Kent. Brother, in regard of thee and of thy land,
Did they remove that flatterer from thy throne.

K. Edw. So, sir, you have spoke: away, avoid our presence!
[*Exit Kent.*
Accursed wretches, was't in regard of us,
When we had sent our messenger to request
He might be spar'd to come to speak with us,
And Pembroke undertook for his return,
That thou, proud Warwick, watch'd the prisoner,
Poor Pierce, and headed him 'gainst law of arms?
For which thy head shall overlook the rest
As much as thou in rage outwent'st the rest.

War. Tyrant, I scorn thy threats and menaces;
It is but temporal that thou canst inflict.

Lan. The worst is death; and better die to live
Than live in infamy under such a king.

K. Edw. Away with them, my lord of Winchester!
These lusty leaders, Warwick and Lancaster,
I charge you roundly, off with both their heads!
Away!

War. Farewell, vain world!

Lan. Sweet Mortimer, farewell!

Y. Mor. England, unkind to thy nobility,
Groan for this grief! behold how thou art maim'd!

K. Edw. Go, take that haughty Mortimer to the Tower;
There see him safe bestow'd; and, for the rest,
Do speedy execution on them all.
Be gone!

Y. Mor. What, Mortimer, can ragged stony walls
Immure thy virtue that aspires to heaven?
No, Edward, England's scourge, it may not be;
Mortimer's hope surmounts his fortune far.
[*The captive Barons are led off.*

K. Edw. Sound, drums and trumpets! March with me, my friends.
Edward this day hath crown'd him king anew.
[*Exeunt all except the younger Spenser,*
Levune and Baldock.

Y. Spen. Levune, the trust that we repose in thee
Begets the quiet of King Edward's land:
Therefore be gone in haste, and with advice
Bestow that treasure on the lords of France,
That, therewith all enchanted, like the guard
That suffer'd Jove to pass in showers of gold
To Danaë, all aid may be denied
To Isabel the queen, that now in France
Makes friends, to cross the seas with her young son,
And step into his father's regiment.

Levune. That's it these barons and the subtle queen
Long levell'd at.

Bal. Yea, but, Levune, thou seest,
These barons lay their heads on blocks together:
What they intend, the hangman frustrates clean.

Levune. Have you no doubt, my lords, I'll clap so close
Among the lords of France with England's gold,
That Isabel shall make her plaints in vain,
And France shall be obdurate with her tears.

Y. Spen. Then make for France amain; Levune, away!
Proclaim King Edward's wars and victories.

[*Exeunt.*

ACT IV.

SCENE I. LONDON, A STREET NEAR THE TOWER

Enter KENT.

Kent. Fair blows the wind for France: blow, gentle gale,
Till Edmund be arriv'd for England's good!
Nature, yield to my country's cause in this!
A brother? no, a butcher of thy friends!
Proud Edward, dost thou banish me thy presence?
But I'll to France, and cheer the wronged queen,
And certify what Edward's looseness is.
Unnatural king, to slaughter nobleman
And cherish flatterers! Mortimer, I stay
Thy sweet escape. Stand gracious, gloomy night,
To his device!

Enter the younger MORTIMER *disguised.*

Y. Mor. Holla! who walketh there?
Is't you, my lord?

Kent. Mortimer, 'tis I.
But hath thy portion wrought so happily?

Y. Mor. It hath, my lord: the warders all asleep,
I thank them, gave me leave to pass in peace.
But hath your grace got shipping unto France?

Kent. Fear it not.

[*Exeunt.*

SCENE II. PARIS.

Enter QUEEN ISABELLA *and* PRINCE EDWARD.

Q. Isab. Ah, boy, our friends do fail us all in France!
The lords are cruel, and the king unkind.
What shall we do?

P. Edw. Madam, return to England,
And please my father well; and then a fig
For all my uncle's friendship here in France!
I warrant you, I'll win his highness quickly;
'A loves me better than a thousand Spensers.

Q. Isab. Ah, boy, thou art deceiv'd, at least in this,
To think that we can yet be tun'd together!
No, no, we jar too far.—Unkind Valois!
Unhappy Isabel, when France rejects,
Whither, O, whither dost thou bend thy steps?

Enter SIR JOHN OF HAINAULT.

Sir J. Madam, what cheer?

Q. Isab. Ah, good Sir John of Hainault,
Never so cheerless nor so far distrest!

Sir J. I hear, sweet lady, of the king's unkindness:
But droop not, madam; noble minds contemn
Despair. Will your grace with me to Hainault,
And there stay time's advantage with your son?—
How say you, my lord! will you go with your friends,
And shake off all our fortunes equally?

P. Edw. So pleaseth the queen my mother, me it likes:
The king of England, not the court of France,
Shall have me from my gracious mother's side,
Till I be strong enough to break a staff;
And then have at the proudest Spenser's head!

Sir J. Well said, my lord!

Q. Isab. O my sweet heart, how do I moan thy wrongs,
Yet triumph in the hope of thee, my joy!—
Ah, sweet Sir John, even to the utmost verge
Of Europe, on the shore of Tanais,

Will we with thee to Hainault—so we will:
The marquis is a noble gentleman;
His grace, I dare presume, will welcome me.—
But who are these?

Enter KENT *and the younger* MORTIMER.

Kent. Madam, long may you live,
Much happier than your friends in England do!

Q. Isab. Lord Edmund and Lord Mortimer alive!
Welcome to France! the news was here, my lord,
That you were dead, or very near your death.

Y. Mor. Lady, the last was truest of the twain:
But Mortimer, reserv'd for better hap,
Hath shaken off the thraldom of the Tower,
And lives t' advance your standard, good my lord.

P. Edw. How mean you, and the king my father lives?
No, my Lord Mortimer, not I, I trow.

Q. Isab. Not, son! Why not? I would it were no worse!—
But, gentle lords, friendless we are in France.

Y. Mor. Monsieur Le Grand, a noble friend of yours,
Told us, at our arrival, all the news,—
How hard the nobles, how unkind the king
Hath show'd himself: but, madam, right makes room
Where weapons want; and, though a many friends
Are made away, as Warwick, Lancaster,
And others of our part and faction,
Yet have we friends, assure your grace, in England,
Would cast up caps, and clap their hands for joy,
To see us there, appointed for our foes.

Kent. Would all were well, and Edward well reclaim'd,
For England's honour, peace, and quietness!

Y. Mor. But by the sword, my lord, 't must be deserv'd:
The king will ne'er forsake his flatterers.

Sir J. My lords of England, sith th' ungentle king
Of France refuseth to give aid of arms
To this distressed queen, his sister, here,
Go you with her to Hainault: doubt ye not
We will find comfort, money, men, and friends,
Ere long to bid the English king a base.—
How say'st, young prince, what think you of the match?

P. Edw. I think King Edward will outrun us all.

Q. Isab. Nay, son, not so; and you must not discourage
Your friends that are so forward in your aid.

Kent. Sir John of Hainault, pardon us, I pray:
These comforts that you give our woful queen
Bind us in kindness all at your command.

Q. Isab. Yea, gentle brother:—and the God of heaven
Prosper your happy motion, good Sir John!

Y. Mor. This noble gentleman, forward in arms,
Was born, I see, to be our anchor-hold.—
Sir John of Hainault, be it thy renown,
That England's queen and nobles in distress
Have been by thee restor'd and comforted.

Sir J. Madam, along; and you, my lord[s], with me,
That England's peers may Hainault's welcome see.

[*Exeunt.*

SCENE III. LONDON, A ROOM IN THE KING'S PALACE.

Enter KING EDWARD, ARUNDEL, *the elder* SPENSER, *the younger* SPENSER, *and others.*

K. Edw. Thus, after many threats of wrathful war,
Triumpheth England's Edward with his friends,
And triumph Edward with his friends uncontroll'd!—
My Lord of Glocester, do you hear the news?

Y. Spen. What news, my lord?

K. Edw. Why, man, they say there is great execution
Done through the realm.—My Lord of Arundel,
You have the note, have you not?

Arun. From the Lieutenant of the Tower, my lord.

K. Edw. I pray, let us see it. [*Takes the note from Arundel.*
—What have we there?—
Read it, Spenser.
[*Gives the note to young Spenser, who reads their names.*

Why, so: they bark'd apace a month ago;
Now, on my life, they'll neither bark nor bite.
Now, sirs, the news from France? Glocester, I trow,
The lords of France love England's gold so well
As Isabella gets no aid from thence.
What now remains? have you proclaim'd, my lord,
Reward for them can bring in Mortimer?

Y. Spen. My lord, we have; and, if he be in England,
'A will be had ere long, I doubt it not.

K. Edw. If, dost thou say? Spenser, as true as death,
He is in England's ground: our port-masters
Are not so careless of their king's command.

Enter a Messenger.

How now! what news with thee? from whence come these?

Mess. Letters, my lord, and tidings forth of France:
To you, my Lord of Glocester, from Levune.
[*Gives letters to young Spenser.*

K. Edw. Read.

Y. Spen. [reading.] *My duty to your honour promised, etc., I have, according to instructions in that behalf, dealt with the King of France and his lords, and effected that the queen, all discontented and discomforted, is gone: whither, if you ask, with Sir John of Hainault, brother to the marquis, into*

Flanders. With them are gone Lord Edmund and the Lord Mortimer, having in their company divers of your nation, and others; and, as constant report goeth, they intend to give King Edward battle in England, sooner than he can look for them. This is all the news of import.
Your honour's in all service, Levune.

K. Edw. Ah, villains, hath that Mortimer escap'd?
With him is Edmund gone associate?
And will Sir John of Hainault lead the round?
Welcome, o' God's name, madam, and your son!
England shall welcome you and all your rout.
Gallop apace, bright Phbus, through the sky;
And, dusky Night, in rusty iron car,
Between you both shorten the time, I pray,
That I may see that most desired day,
When we may meet these traitors in the field!
Ah, nothing grieves me, but my little boy
Is thus misled to countenance their ills!
Come, friends, to Bristow, there to make us strong:
And, winds, as equal be to bring them in,
As you injurious were to bear them forth!

[*Exeunt.*

SCENE IV. THE QUEEN'S CAMP, NEAR OR-WELL, SUFFOLK.

Enter QUEEN ISABELLA, PRINCE EDWARD, KENT, *the younger* MORTIMER, *and* SIR JOHN OF HAINAULT.

Q. Isab. Now, lords, our loving friends and countrymen,
Welcome to England all, with prosperous winds!
Our kindest friends in Belgia have we left,
To cope with friends at home; a heavy case
When force to force is knit, and sword and glaive
In civil broils make kin and countrymen
Slaughter themselves in others, and their sides
With their own weapons gor'd! But what's the help?
Misgovern'd kings are cause of all this wreck;
And, Edward, thou art one among them all,
Whose looseness hath betray'd thy land to spoil,
Who made the channel overflow with blood
Of thine own people: patron shouldst thou be;
But thou—

Y. Mor. Nay, madam, if you be a warrior,
You must not grow so passionate in speeches.—
Lords, sith that we are, by sufferance of heaven,
Arriv'd and armed in this prince's right,
Here for our country's cause swear we to him
All homage, fealty, and forwardness;
And for the open wrongs and injuries
Edward hath done to us, his queen, and land,
We come in arms to wreck it with the sword;
That England's queen in peace may repossess
Her dignities and honours; and withal
We may remove these flatterers from the king
That havock England's wealth and treasury.

Sir J. Sound trumpets, my lord, and forward let us march.
Edward will think we come to flatter him.

Kent. I would he never had been flatter'd more!

[*Exeunt.*

SCENE V. NEAR BRISTOL.

Enter KING EDWARD, BALDOCK, *and the younger* SPENSER.

Y. Spen. Fly, fly, my lord! the queen is overstrong;
Her friends do multiply, and yours do fail.
Shape we our course to Ireland, there to breathe.

K. Edw. What, was I born to fly and run away,
And leave the Mortimers conquerors behind?
Give me my horse, and let's reinforce our troops.
And in this bed of honour die with fame.

Bald. O, no, my lord! this princely resolution
Fits not the time: away! we are pursu'd. [*Exeunt.*

Enter KENT, *with a sword and target.*

Kent. This way he fled; but I am come too late.
Edward, alas, my heart relents for thee!
Proud traitor, Mortimer, why dost thou chase
Thy lawful king, thy sovereign, with thy sword?
Vile wretch, and why hast thou, of all unkind,
Borne arms against thy brother and thy king?
Rain showers of vengeance on my cursed head,
Thou God, to whom in justice it belongs
To punish this unnatural revolt!
Edward, this Mortimer aims at thy life:
O, fly him, then! But, Edmund, calm this rage;
Dissemble, or thou diest; for Mortimer
And Isabel do kiss, while they conspire:
And yet she bears a face of love, forsooth:
Fie on that love that hatcheth death and hate!
Edmund, away! Bristow to Longshanks' blood
Is false; be not found single for suspect:
Proud Mortimer pries near into thy walks.

Enter QUEEN ISABELLA, PRINCE EDWARD, *the younger*
MORTIMER, *and* SIR JOHN JOHN OF HAINAULT.

Q. Isab. Successful battle gives the God of kings
To them that fight in right, and fear in wrath,
Since, then, successfully we have prevail'd,
Thanked be heaven's great architect, and you!

Ere farther we proceed, my noble lords,
We here create our well-beloved son,
Of love and care unto his royal person,
Lord Warden of the realm; and, sith the Fates
Have made his father so infortunate,
Deal you, my lords, in this, my loving lords,
As to your wisdoms fittest seems in all.

Kent. Madam, without offence if I may ask
How will you deal with Edward in his fall?

P. Edw. Tell me, good uncle, what Edward do you mean?

Kent. Nephew, your father; I dare not call him king.

Y. Mor. My Lord of Kent, what needs these questions?
'Tis not in her controlment nor in ours;
But as the realm and parliament shall please,
So shall your brother be disposed of.—
I like not this relenting mood in Edmund:
Madam, 'tis good to look to him betimes. [*Aside to the Queen.*

Q. Isab. My lord, the Mayor of Bristow knows our mind.

Y. Mor. Yea, madam; and they scape not easily
That fled the field.

Q. Isab. Baldock is with the king:
A goodly chancellor, is he not, my lord?

Sir J. So are the Spensers, the father and the son.

Y. Mor. This Edward is the ruin of the realm.

Enter RICE AP HOWEL *with the elder* SPENSER *prisoner,
and* Attendants.

Rice. God save Queen Isabel and her princely son!
Madam, the Mayor and citizens of Bristow,
In sign of love and duty to this presence,
Present by me this traitor to the state,
Spenser, the father to that wanton Spenser,
That, like the lawless Catiline of Rome,
Revell'd in England's wealth and treasury.

Isab. We thank you all.

Y. Mor. Your loving care in this
Deserveth princely favours and rewards.
But where's the king and the other Spenser fled?

Rice. Spenser the son, created Earl of Glocester,
Is with that smooth-tongu'd scholar Baldock gone,
And shipp'd but late for Ireland with the king.

Y. Mor. Some whirlwind fetch them back, or sink them all!— [*Aside.*

They shall be started thence, I doubt it not.

P. Edw. Shall I not see the king my father yet?

Kent. Unhappy Edward, chas'd from England's bounds! [*Aside.*

Sir J. Madam, what resteth? why stand you in a muse?

Q. Isab. I rue my lord's ill-fortune: but, alas,
Care of my country call'd me to this war!

Y. Mor. Madam, have done with care and sad complaint:
Your king hath wrong'd your country and himself,
And we must seek to right it as we may. —
Meanwhile have hence this rebel to the block.

E. Spen. Rebel is he that fights against the prince:
So fought not they that fought in Edward's right.

Y. Mor. Take him away; he prates.
[*Exeunt Attendants with the elder Spenser.*
You, Rice ap Howel,
Shall do good service to her majesty,
Being of countenance in your country here,
To follow these rebellious runagates. —
We in mean while, madam, must take advice.
How Baldock, Spenser, and their complices,
May in their fall be follow'd to their end.

[*Exeunt.*

SCENE VI. WITHIN THE ABBEY OF NEATH.

Enter the Abbot, Monks, KING EDWARD, *the younger* SPENSER, *and* BALDOCK (*the three latter disguised*).

Abbot. Have you no doubt, my lord; have you no fear:
As silent and as careful we will be
To keep your royal person safe with us,
Free from suspect, and fell invasion
Of such as have your majesty in chase,
Yourself, and those your chosen company,
As danger of this stormy time requires.

K. Edw. Father, thy face should harbour no deceit.
O, hadst thou ever been a king, thy heart,
Pierc'd deeply with sense of my distress,
Could not but take compassion of my state!
Stately and proud in riches and in train,
Whilom I was, powerful and full of pomp:
But what is he whom rule and empery
Have not in life or death made miserable?—
Come, Spenser,—come, Baldock,—come, sit down by me;
Make trial now of that philosophy
That in our famous nurseries of arts
Thou suck'dst from Plato and from Aristotle.—
Father, this life contemplative is heaven:
O, that I might this life in quiet lead!
But we, alas, are chas'd!—and you, my friends,
Your lives and my dishonour they pursue.—
Yet, gentle monks, for treasure, gold, nor fee,
Do you betray us and our company.

First Monk. Your grace may sit secure, if none but we
Do wot of your abode.

Y. Spen. Not one alive: but shrewdly I suspect
A gloomy fellow in a mead below;
'A gave a long look after us, my lord;
And all the land, I know, is up in arms,
Arms that pursue our lives with deadly hate.

Bald. We were embark'd for Ireland; wretched we,
With awkward winds and with sore tempests driven,

To fall on shore, and here to pine in fear
Of Mortimer and his confederates!

K. Edw. Mortimer! who talks of Mortimer?
Who wounds me with the name of Mortimer,
That bloody man?—Good father, on thy lap
Lay I this head, laden with mickle care.
O, might I never ope these eyes again,
Never again lift up this drooping head,
O, never more lift up this dying heart!

Y. Spen. Look up, my lord.—Baldock, this drowsiness
Betides no good; here even we are betray'd.

Enter, with Welsh hooks, RICE AP HOWEL, *a* Mower,
and LEICESTER.

Mow. Upon my life, these be the men ye seek.

Rice. Fellow, enough.—My lord, I pray, be short;
A fair commission warrants what we do.

Leices. The queen's commission, urg'd by Mortimer:
What cannot gallant Mortimer with the queen?—
Alas, see where he sits, and hopes unseen
T'escape their hands that seek to reave his life!
Too true it is, *Quem dies vidit veniens superbum,*
Hunc dies vidit fugiens jacentem.
But, Leicester, leave to grow so passionate.—
Spenser and Baldock, by no other names,
I arrest you of high treason here.
Stand not on titles, but obey th' arrest:
'Tis in the name of Isabel the queen.—
My lord, why droop you thus?

K. Edw. O day, the last of all my bliss on earth!
Centre of all misfortune! O my stars,
Why do you lour unkindly on a king?
Comes Leicester, then, in Isabella's name,
To take my life, my company from me?
Here, man, rip up this panting breast of mine,
And take my heart in rescue of my friends.

Rice. Away with them!

Y. Spen. It may become thee yet
To let us take our farewell of his grace.

Abbott. My heart with pity earns to see this sight;
A king to bear these words and proud commands! [*Aside.*

K. Edw. Spenser, ah, sweet Spenser, thus, then, must we part?

Y. Spen. We must, my lord; so will the angry heavens.

K. Edw. Nay, so will hell and cruel Mortimer:
The gentle heavens have not to do in this.

Bald. My lord, it is in vain to grieve or storm.
Here humbly of your grace we take our leaves:
Our lots are cast; I fear me, so is thine.

K. Edw. In heaven we may, in earth ne'er shall we meet:—
And, Leicester, say, what shall become of us?

Leices. Your majesty must go to Killingworth.

K. Edw. Must! it is somewhat hard when kings must go.

Leices. Here is a litter ready for your grace,
That waits your pleasure, and the day grows old.

Rice. As good be gone, as stay and be benighted.

K. Edw. A litter hast thou? lay me in a hearse,
And to the gates of hell convey me hence;
Let Pluto's bells ring out my fatal knell,
And hags howl for my death at Charon's shore;
For friends hath Edward none but these,
And these must die under a tyrant's sword.

Rice. My lord, be going: care not for these;
For we shall see them shorter by the heads.

K. Edw. Well, that shall be shall be: part we must;
Sweet Spenser, gentle Baldock, part we must.—
Hence, feigned weeds! unfeigned are my woes.—
[*Throwing off his disguise.*
Father, farewell.—Leicester, thou stay'st for me;
And go I must.—Life, farewell, with my friends!
[*Exeunt King Edward and Leicester.*

Y. Spen. O, is he gone? is noble Edward gone?
Parted from hence, never to see us more!
Rend, sphere of heaven! and, fire, forsake thy orb!
Earth, melt to air! gone is my sovereign,
Gone, gone, alas, never to make return!

Bald. Spenser, I see our souls are fleeting hence;
We are depriv'd the sunshine of our life.
Make for a new life, man; throw up thy eyes
And heart and hand to heaven's immortal throne;
Pay nature's debt with cheerful countenance;
Reduce we all our lessons unto this,—
To die, sweet Spenser, therefore live we all;
Spenser, all live to die, and rise to fall.

Rice. Come, come, keep these preachments till you come to
the place appointed. You, and such as you are, have

made wise work in England. Will your lordships away?

Mow. Your lordship I trust will remember me?

Rice. Remember thee, fellow! what else? Follow me to the town.

[*Exeunt.*

ACT V.

SCENE I. KILLINGWORTH CASTLE.

Enter KING EDWARD, LEICESTER, *the* BISHOP OF
WINCHESTER, *and* TRUSSEL.

Leices. Be patient, good my lord, cease to lament;
Imagine Killingworth Castle were your court,
And that you lay for pleasure here a space,
Not of compulsion or necessity.

K. Edw. Leicester, if gentle words might comfort me,
Thy speeches long ago had eas'd my sorrows,
For kind and loving hast thou always been.
The griefs of private men are soon allay'd;
But not of kings. The forest deer, being struck,
Runs to an herb that closeth up the wounds:
But when the imperial lion's flesh is gor'd,
He rends and tears it with his wrathful paw,
[And], highly scorning that the lowly earth
Should drink his blood, mounts up to the air:
And so it fares with me, whose dauntless mind
Th' ambitious Mortimer would seek to curb,
And that unnatural queen, false Isabel,
That thus hath pent and mew'd me in a prison
For such outrageous passions cloy my soul,
As with the wings of rancour and disdain
Full oft[ten] am I soaring up to heaven,
To plain me to the gods against them both.
But when I call to mind I am a king,
Methinks I should revenge me of my wrongs,
That Mortimer and Isabel have done.
But what are kings, when regiment is gone,
But perfect shadows in a sunshine day?
My nobles rule; I bear the name of king,
I wear the crown; but am controll'd by them,
By Mortimer, and my unconstant queen,
Who spots my nuptial bed with infamy;
Whilst I am lodg'd within this cave of care,
Where sorrow at my elbow still attends,
To company my heart with sad laments,
That bleeds within me for this strange exchange.

But tell me, must I now resign my crown,
To make usurping Mortimer a king?

Bish. of Win. Your grace mistakes; it is for England's good,
And princely Edward's right, we crave the crown.

K. Edw. No, 'tis for Mortimer, not Edward's head
For he's a lamb, emcompassed by wolves,
Which in a moment will abridge his life.
But, if proud Mortimer do wear this crown,
Heavens turn it to a blaze of quenchless fire!
Or, like the snaky wreath of Tisiphon,
Engirt the temples of his hateful head!
So shall not England's vine be perished,
But Edward's name survive, though Edward dies.

Leices. My lord, why waste you thus the time away?
They stay your answer: will you yield your crown?

K. Edw. Ah, Leicester, weigh how hardly I can brook
To lose my crown and kingdom without cause;
To give ambitious Mortimer my right,
That, like a mountain, overwhelms my bliss;
In which extreme my mind here murder'd is!
But that the heavens appoint I must obey. —
Here, take my crown; the life of Edward too: [*Taking off the crown.*
Two kings in England cannot reign at once.
But stay a while: let me be king till night,
That I may gaze upon this glittering crown;
So shall my eyes receive their last content,
My head, the latest honour due to it,
And jointly both yield up their wished right.
Continue ever, thou celestial sun;
Let never silent night possess this clime;
Stand still, you watches of the element;
All times and seasons, rest you at a stay,
That Edward may be still fair England's king!
But day's bright beams doth vanish fast away,
And needs I must resign my wished crown.
Inhuman creatures, nurs'd with tiger's milk,
Why gape you for your sovereign's overthrow?
My diadem, I mean, and guiltless life.
See, monsters, see! I'll wear my crown again.
[*Putting on the crown.*
What, fear you not the fury of your king? —
But, hapless Edward, thou art fondly led;
They pass not for thy frowns as late they did,
But seek to make a new-elected king;
Which fills my mind with strange despairing thoughts,

Which thoughts are martyred with endless torments;
And in this torment comfort find I none,
But that I feel the crown upon my head;
And therefore let me wear it yet a while.

Trus. My, lord, the parliament must have present news;
And therefore say, will you resign or no?
[*The king rageth.*

K. Edw. I'll not resign, but, whilst I live, [be king].
Traitors, be gone, and join you with Mortimer.
Elect, conspire, install, do what you will:
Their blood and yours shall seal these treacheries.

Bish. of Win. This answer we'll return; and so, farewell.
[*Going with Trussel.*

Leices. Call them again, my lord, and speak them fair;
For, if they go, the prince shall lose his right.

K. Edw. Call thou them back; I have no power to speak.

Leices. My lord, the king is willing to resign.

Bish. of Win. If he be not, let him choose.

K. Edw. O, would I might! but heavens and earth conspire
To make me miserable. Here, receive my crown.
Receive it? no, these innocent hands of mine
Shall not be guilty of so foul a crime;
He of you all that most desires my blood,
And will be call'd the murderer of a king,
Take it. What, are you mov'd? pity you me?
Then send for unrelenting Mortimer,
And Isabel, whose eyes being turn'd to steel
Will sooner sparkle fire than shed a tear.
Yet stay; for, rather than I'll look on them,
Here, here! [*Gives the crown.*]—Now, sweet God of heaven,
Make me despise this transitory pomp,
And sit fot aye enthronised in heaven!
Come, death, and with thy fingers close my eyes,
Or, if I live, let me forget myself!

Bish. of Win. My lord,—

K. Edw. Call me not lord; away, out of my sight!
Ah, pardon me! grief makes me lunatic.
Let not that Mortimer protect my son;
More safety there is in a tiger's jaws
Than his embracements. Bear this to the queen,
Wet with my tears, and dried again with sighs:
[*Gives a handkerchief.*
If with the sight thereof she be not mov'd,

Return it back, and dip it in my blood.
Commend me to my son, and bid him rule
Better than I: yet how have I transgress'd,
Unless it be with too much clemency?

Trus. And thus, most humbly do we take our leave.

K. Edw. Farewell.
[*Exeunt the Bishop of Winchester and Trussel with the
crown.*
I know the next news that they bring
Will be my death; and welcome shall it be:
To wretched men death is felicity.

Leices. Another post! what news brings he?

Enter BERKELEY, *who gives a paper to* LEICESTER.

K. Edw. Such news as I expect.—Come, Berkeley, come,
And tell thy message to my naked breast.

Berk. My lord, think not a thought so villanous
Can harbour in a man of noble birth.
To do your highness service and devoir,
And save you from your foes,
Berkeley would die.

Leices. My lord, the council of the queen command
That I resign my charge.

K. Edw. And who must keep me now?
Must you, my lord?

Berk. Ay, my most gracious lord; so 'tis decreed.

K. Edw.
[*Taking the paper.*]
By Mortimer, whose name is written here!
Well may I rent his name that rends my heart.
[*Tears it.*
This poor revenge hath something eas'd my mind:
So may his limbs be torn as is this paper!
Hear me, immortal Jove, and grant it too!

Berk. Your grace must hence with me to Berkeley straight.

K. Edw. Whither you will: all places are alike,
And every earth is fit for burial.

Leices. Favour him, my lord, as much as lieth in you.

Berk. Even so betide my soul as I use him!

K. Edw. Mine enemy hath pitied my estate,
And that's the cause that I am now remov'd.

Berk. And thinks your grace that Berkeley will be cruel?

K. Edw. I know not; but of this am I assur'd,
That death ends all, and I can die but once.— Leicester, farewell.

Leices. Not yet, my lord; I'll bear you on your way.

[*Exeunt.*

SCENE II. WESTMINSTER, A ROOM IN THE PALACE.

Enter QUEEN ISABELLA *and the younger* MORTIMER.

Y. Mor. Fair Isabel, now have we our desire;
The proud corrupters of the light-brain'd king
Have done their homage to the lofty gallows,
And he himself lies in captivity.
Be rul'd by me, and we will rule the realm:
In any case take heed of childish fear,
For now we hold an old wolf by the ears,
That, if he slip, will seize upon us both,
And gripe the sorer, being grip'd himself.
Think therefore, madam, that imports us much
To erect your son with all the speed we may,
And that I be protector over him:
For our behoof, 'twill bear the greater sway
Whenas a king's name shall be under-writ.

Q. Isab. Sweet Mortimer, the life of Isabel,
Be thou persuaded that I love thee well;
And therefore, so the prince my son be safe,
Whom I esteem as dear as these mine eyes,
Conclude against his father what thou wilt,
And I myself will willingly subscribe.

Y. Mor. First would I hear news he were depos'd,
And then let me alone to handle him.

Enter Messenger.

Letters! from whence? *Mess.* From Killingworth, my lord? *Q. Isab.* How
fares my lord the king? *Mess.* In health, madam, but full of pensiveness.
Q. Isab. Alas, poor soul, would I could ease his grief!

Enter the BISHOP OF WINCHESTER *with the crown.*

Thanks, gentle Winchester. —
Sirrah, be gone. [*Exit Messenger.*

Bish. of Win. The king hath willingly resign'd his crown.

Q. Isab. O, happy news! send for the prince my son.

Bish. of Win. Further, or this letter was seal'd, Lord Berkeley came,
So that he now is gone from Killingworth;
And we have heard that Edmund laid a plot
To set his brother free; nor more but so.
The Lord of Berkeley is so pitiful
As Leicester that had charge of him before.

Q. Isab. Then let some other be his guardian.

Y. Mor. Let me alone; here is the privy-seal, —
[*Exit the Bish. of Win.*
Who's there? Call hither, Gurney and Matrevis. —
[*To Attendants within.*
To dash the heavy-headed Edmund's drift,
Berkeley shall be discharg'd, the king remov'd,
And none but we shall know where he lieth.

Q. Isab. But, Mortimer, as long as he survives,
What safety rests for us or for my son?

Y. Mor. Speak, shall he presently be despatch'd and die?

Q. Isab. I would he were, so 'twere not by my means!

Enter MATREVIS *and* GURNEY.

Y. Mor. Enough. — Matrevis, write a letter presently
Unto the Lord of Berkeley from ourself,
That he resign the king to thee and Gurney;
And, when 'tis done, we will subscribe our name.

Mat. It shall be done, my lord. [*Writes.*

Y. Mor. Gurney, —

Gur. My lord?

Y. Mor. As thou intend'st to rise by Mortimer,
Who now makes Fortune's wheel turn as he please,
Seek all the means thou canst to make him droop,
And neither give him kind word nor good look.

Gur. I warrant you, my lord.

Y. Mor. And this above the rest: because we hear
That Edmund casts to work his liberty,
Remove him still from place to place by night,
Till at the last he come to Killingworth,
And then from thence to Berkeley back again;
And by the way, to make him fret the more,
Speak curstly to him; and in any case
Let no man comfort him, if he chance to weep,
But amplify his grief with bitter words.

Mat. Fear not, my lord; we'll do as you command.

Y. Mor. So, now away! post thitherwards amain.

Q. Isab. Whither goes this letter? to my lord the king?
Commend me humbly to his majesty,
And tell him that I labour all in vain
To ease his grief and work his liberty;
And bear him this as witness of my love. [*Gives ring.*

Mat. I will, madam. [*Exit with Gurney.*

Y. Mor. Finely dissembled! do so still, sweet queen.
Here comes the young prince with the Earl of Kent.

Q. Isab. Something he whispers in his childish ears.

Y. Mor. If he have such access unto the prince,
Our plots and stratagems will soon be dash'd.

Q. Isab. Use Edmund friendly, as if all were well.

Enter PRINCE EDWARD, *and* KENT *talking with him.*

Y. Mor. How fares my honourable Lord of Kent?

Kent. In health, sweet Mortimer.—How fares your grace?

Q. Isab. Well, if my lord your brother were enlarg'd.

Kent. I hear of late he hath depos'd himself.

Q. Isab. The more my grief.

Y. Mor. And mine.

Kent. Ah, they do dissemble!

[*Aside.*

Q. Isab. Sweet son, come hither; I must talk with thee.

Y. Mor. You, being his uncle and the next of blood,
Do look to be protector o'er the prince.

Kent. Not I, my lord: who should protect the son,
But she that gave him life?
I mean the queen.

P. Edw. Mother, persuade me not to wear the crown:
Let him be king; I am too young to reign.

Q. Isab. But be content, seeing 'tis his highness' pleasure.

P. Edw. Let me but see him first, and then I will.

Kent. Ay, do, sweet nephew.

Q. Isab. Brother, you know it is impossible.

P. Edw. Why, is he dead?

Q. Isab. No, God forbid!

Kent. I would those words proceeded from your heart!

Y. Mor. Inconstant Edmund, dost thou favour him,
That wast a cause of his imprisonment?

Kent. The more cause now have I to make amends.

Y. Mor. [*aside to* Q. ISAB.] I tell thee, 'tis not meet that one so false
Should come about the person of a prince.—
My lord, he hath betray'd the king his brother,
And therefore trust him not.

P. Edw. But he repents, and sorrows for it now.

Q. Isab. Come, son, and go with this gentle lord and me.

P. Edw. With you I will, but not with Mortimer.

Y. Mor. Why, youngling, 'sdain'st thou so of Mortimer?
Then I will carry thee by force away.

P. Edw. Help, uncle Kent! Mortimer will wrong me.

Q. Isab. Brother Edmund, strive not; we are his friends;
Isabel is nearer than the Earl of Kent.

Kent. Sister, Edward is my charge; redeem him.

Q. Isab. Edward is my son, and I will keep him.

Kent. Mortimer shall know that he hath wronged me.
Hence will I haste to Killingworth Castle,
And rescue aged Edward from his foes,
To be reveng'd on Mortimer and thee.

[*Aside.*

[*Exeunt, on the one side, Queen Isabella, Prince Edward and the younger Mortimer; on other other, Kent.*

SCENE III. NEAR KILLINGWORTH CASTLE.

Enter MATREVIS, GURNEY, *and* Soldiers, *with*
KING EDWARD.

Mat. My lord, be not pensive; we are your friends:
Men are ordain'd to live in misery;
Therefore, come; dalliance dangereth our lives.

K. Edw. Friends, whither must unhappy Edward go?
Will hateful Mortimer appoint no rest?
Must I be vexed like the nightly bird,
Whose sight is loathsome to all winged fowls?
When will the fury of his mind assuage?
When will his heart be satisfied with blood?
If mine will serve, unbowel straight this breast,
And give my heart to Isabel and him:
It is the chiefest mark they level at.

Gur. Not so, my liege: the queen hath given this charge,
To keep your grace in safety:
Your passions make your dolours to increase.

K. Edw. This usage makes my misery increase.
But can my air of life continue long,
When all my senses are annoy'd with stench?
Within a dungeon England's king is kept,
Where I am starv'd for want of sustenance;
My daily diet is heart-breaking sobs,
That almost rent the closet of my heart:
Thus lives old Edward not reliev'd by any,
And so must die, though pitied by many.
O, water, gentle friends, to cool my thirst,
And clear my body from foul excrements!

Mat. Here's channel-water, as our charge is given:
Sit down, for we'll be barbers to your grace.

K. Edw. Traitors, away! what, will you murder me,
Of choke your sovereign with puddle-water?

Gur. No, but wash your face, and shave away your beard,
Lest you be known, and so be rescued.

Mat. Why strive you thus? your labour is in vain.

K. Edw. The wren may strive against the lion's strength,
But all in vain: so vainly do I strive
To seek for mercy at a tyrant's hand.
[*They wash him with puddle-water, and shave his beard away.*
Immortal powers, that know the painful cares
That wait upon my poor distressed soul,
O, level all your looks upon these daring men
That wrong their liege and sovereign, England's king!
O Gaveston, it is for thee that I am wrong'd!
For me both thou and both the Spensers died;
And for your sakes a thousand wrongs I'll take.
The Spensers' ghosts, wherever they remain,
Wish well to mine; then, tush, for them I'll die.

Mat. 'Twixt theirs and yours shall be no enmity.
Come, come, away! Now put the torches out:
We'll enter in by darkness to Killingworth.

Gur. How now! who comes there?

Enter KENT.

Mat. Guard the king sure: it is the Earl of Kent.

K. Edw. O gentle brother, help to rescue me!

Mat. Keep them asunder; thrust in the king.

Kent. Soldiers, let me but talk to him one word.

Gur. Lay hands upon the earl for his assault.

Kent. Lay down your weapons, traitors! yield the king!

Mat. Edmund, yield thou thyself, or thou shalt die.

Kent. Base villains, wherefore do you gripe me thus?

Gur. Bind him, and so convey him to the court.

Kent. Where is the court but here? here is the king
And I will visit him: why stay you me?

Mat. The court is where Lord Mortimer remains:
Thither shall your honour go; and so, farewell.

[*Exeunt Matrevis and Gurney with King Edward.*

Kent. O, miserable is that common-weal,
Where lords keep courts, and kings are lock'd in prison!

First Sold. Wherefore stay we? on, sirs, to the court!

Kent. Ay, lead me whither you will, even to my death,
Seeing that my brother cannot be releas'd.

[*Exeunt.*

SCENE IV. WESTMINSTER, A ROOM IN THE PALA.

Enter the younger MORTIMER.

Y. Mor. The king must die, or Mortimer goes down;
The commons now begin to pity him:
Yet he that is the cause of Edward's death,
Is sure to pay for it when his son's of age;
And therefore will I do it cunningly.
This letter, written by a friend of ours,
Contains his death, yet bids then save his life;
[*Reads.*
Edwardum occidere nolite timere, bonum est,
Fear not to kill the king, 'tis good he die:
But read it thus, and that's another sense;
Edwardum occidere nolite, timere bonum est,
Kill not the king, ‹tis good to fear the worst.
Unpointed as it is, thus shall it go.
That, being dead, if it chance to be found,
Matrevis and the rest may bear the blame,
And we be quit that caus'd it to be done.
Within this room is lock'd the messenger
That shall convey it, and perform the rest;
And, by a secret token that he bears,
Shall he be murder'd when the deed is done. —
Lightborn, come forth!

Enter LIGHTBORN.

Art thou so resolute as thou wast?

Light. What else, my lord? and far more resolute.

Y. Mor. And hast thou cast how to accomplish it?

Light. Ay, ay; and none shall know which way he died.

Y. Mor. But at his looks, Lightborn, thou wilt relent.

Light. Relent! ha, ha! I use much to relent.

Y. Mor. Well, do it bravely, and be secret.

Light. You shall not need to give instructions;

'Tis not the first time I have kill'd a man:
I learn'd in Naples how to poison flowers;
To strangle with a lawn thrust down the throat;
To pierce the wind pipe with a needle's point;
Or, whilst one is asleep, to take a quill,
And blow a little powder in his ears;
Or open his mouth, and pour quick-silver down.
But yet I have a braver way than these.

Y. Mor. What's that?

Light. Nay, you shall pardon me; none shall know my tricks.

Y. Mor. I care not how it is, so it be not spied.
Deliver this to Gurney and Matrevis: [*Gives letter.*
At every ten-mile end thou hast a horse:
Take this [*Gives money*]: away, and never see me more!

Light. No?

Y. Mor. No; unless thou bring me news of Edward's death.

Light. That will I quickly do. Farewell, my lord. [*Exit.*

Y. Mor. The prince I rule, the queen do I command,
And with a lowly congé to the ground
The proudest lords salute me as I pass;
I seal, I cancel, I do what I will.
Fear'd am I more than lov'd;—let me be fear'd,
And, when I frown, make all the court look pale.
I view the prince with Aristarchus' eyes,
Whose looks were as a breeching to a boy.
They thrust upon me the protectorship,
And sue to me for that that I desire;
While at the council-table, grave enough,
And not unlike a bashful puritan,
First I complain of imbecility,
Saying it is *onus quam gravissimum;*
Till, being interrupted by my friends,
Suscepi that *provinciam*, as they term it;
And, to conclude, I am Protector now.
Now all is sure: the queen and Mortimer
Shall rule the realm, the king; and none rule us.
Mine enemies will I plague, my friends advance;
And what I list command who dare control?
Major sum quàm cui possit fortuna nocere:
And that this be the coronation-day,
It pleaseth me and Isabel the queen. [*Trumpets within.*
The trumpets sound; I must go take my place.

Enter KING EDWARD THE THIRD, QUEEN ISABELLA, *the*

ARCHBISHOP OF CANTERBURY, Champion, *and* Nobles.

Archb. of Cant. Long live King Edward, by the grace of God
King of England and Lord of Ireland!

Cham. If any Christian, Heathen, Turk, or Jew,
Dares but affirm that Edward's not true king,
And will avouch his saying with the sword,
I am the Champion that will combat him.

Y. Mor. None comes: sound, trumpets!

[*Trumpets.*
K. Edw. Third. Champion, here's to thee.

[*Gives purse.*
Q. Isab. Lord Mortimer, now take him to your charge.

Enter Soldiers *with* KENT *prisoner.*

Y. Mor. What traitor have we there with blades and bills?

First Sold. Edmund the Earl of Kent.

K. Edw. Third. What hath he done?

First Sold. 'A would have taken the king away perforce,
As we were bringing him to Killingworth.

Y. Mor. Did you attempt his rescue, Edmund? speak.

Kent. Mortimer, I did: he is our king,
And thou compell'st this prince to wear the crown.

Y. Mor. Strike off his head: he shall have martial law.

Kent. Strike off my head! base traitor, I defy thee!

K. Edw. Third. My lord, he is my uncle, and shall live.

Y. Mor. My lord, he is your enemy, and shall die.

Kent. Stay, villains!

K. Edw. Third. Sweet mother, if I cannot pardon him,
Entreat my Lord Protector for his life.

Q. Isab. Son, be content: I dare not speak a word.

K. Edw. Third. Nor I; and yet methinks I should command:
But, seeing I cannot, I'll entreat for him.—
My lord, if you will let my uncle live,
I will requite it when I come to age.

Y. Mor. 'Tis for your highness' good and for the realm's.—
How often shall I bid you bear him hence?

Kent. Art thou king? must I die at thy command?

Y. Mor. At our command.—Once more, away with him!

Kent. Let me but stay and speak; I will not go:

Either my brother or his son is king,
And none of both them thirst for Edmund's blood:
And therefore, soldiers, whither will you hale me?

[*Soldiers hale Kent away, and carry him to be beheaded.*

K. Edw. Third. What safety may I look for at his hands,
If that my uncle shall be murder'd thus?

Q. Isab. Fear not, sweet boy;
I'll guard thee from thy foes:
Had Edmund liv'd, he would have sought thy death.
Come, son, we'll ride a-hunting in the park.

K. Edw. Third. And shall my uncle Edmund ride with us?

Q. Isab. He is a traitor; think not on him: come.

[*Exeunt.*

SCENE V. A ROOM IN BERKELEY CASTLE.

Enter MATREVIS *and* GURNEY.

Mat. Gurney, I wonder the king dies not,
Being in a vault up to the knees in water,
To which the channels of the castle run,
From whence a damp continually ariseth,
That were enough to poison any man,
Much more a king, brought up so tenderly.

Gur. And so do I, Matrevis: yesternight
I open'd but the door to throw him meat,
And I was almost stifled with the savour.

Mat. He hath a body able to endure
More than we can inflict: and therefore now
Let us assail his mind another while.

Gur. Send for him out thence, and I will anger him.

Mat. But stay; who's this?

Enter LIGHTBORN.

Light. My Lord Protector greets you. [*Gives letter.*

Gur. What's there? I know not how to construe it.

Mat. Gurney, it was left unpointed for the nonce;
Edwardum occidere nolite timere,
That's his meaning.

Light. Know you this token? I must have the king. [*Gives token.*

Mat. Ay, stay a while; thou shalt have answer straight.—
This villain's sent to make away the king.

Gur. I thought as much.

Mat. And, when the murder's done,
See how he must be handled for his labour,—
Pereat iste! Let him have the king;
What else?—Here is the keys, this is the lake:
Do as you are commanded by my lord.

Light. I know what I must do. Get you away:
Yet be not far off; I shall need your help:

See that in the next room I have a fire,
And get me a spit, and let it be red-hot.

Mat. Very well.

Gur. Need you anything besides?

Light. What else? a table and a feather-bed.

Gur. That's all?

Light. Ay, ay: so, when I call you, bring it in.

Mat. Fear not thou that.

Gur. Here's a light to go into the dungeon.
[*Gives light to Lightborn, and then exit with Matrevis.*

Light. So, now.
Must I about this gear: ne'er was there any
So finely handled as this king shall be. —
Foh, here's a place indeed with all my heart!

K. Edw. Who's there? what light is that? wherefore com'st thou?

Light. To comfort you, and bring you joyful news.

K. Edw. Small comfort finds poor Edward in thy looks:
Villain, I know thou com'st to murder me.

Light. To murder you, my most gracious lord?
Far is it from my heart to do you harm.
The queen sent me to see how you were us'd,
For she relents at this your misery:
And what eye can refrain from shedding tears,
To see a king in this most piteous state?

K. Edw. Weep'st thou already? list a while to me,
And then thy heart, were it as Gurney's is,
Or as Matrevis', hewn from the Caucasus,
Yet will it melt ere I have done my tale.
This dungeon where they keep me is the sink
Wherein the filth of all the castle falls.

Light. O villains!

K. Edw. And there, in mire and puddle, have I stood
This ten days' space; and, lest that I should sleep,
One plays continually upon a drum;
They give me bread and water, being a king;
So that, for want of sleep and sustenance,
My mind's distemper'd, and my body's numb'd,
And whether I have limbs or no I know not.
O, would my blood dropp'd out from every vein,
As doth this water from my tatter'd robes!
Tell Isabel the queen, I look'd not thus,

When for her sake I ran at tilt in France,
And there unhors'd the Duke of Cleremont.

Light. O, speak no more, my lord! this breaks my heart.
Lie on this bed, and rest yourself a while.

K. Edw. These looks of thine can harbour naught but death;
I see my tragedy written in thy brows.
Yet stay a while; forbear thy bloody hand,
And let me see the stroke before it comes,
That even then when I shall lose my life,
My mind may be more steadfast on my God.

Light. What means your highness to mistrust me thus?

K. Edw. What mean'st thou to dissemble with me thus?

Light. These hands were never stain'd with innocent blood,
Nor shall they now be tainted with a king's.

K. Edw. Forgive my thought for having such a thought.
One jewel have I left; receive thou this: [*Gives jewel.*
Still fear I, and I know not what's the cause,
But every joint shakes as I give it thee.
O, if thou harbour'st murder in thy heart,
Let this gift change thy mind, and save thy soul!
Know that I am a king: O, at that name
I feel a hell of grief! where is my crown?
Gone, gone! and do I [still] remain alive?

Light. You're overwatch'd, my lord: lie down and rest.

K. Edw. But that grief keeps me waking, I should sleep;
For not these ten days have these eye-lids clos'd.
Now, as I speak, they fall; and yet with fear
Open again. O, wherefore sitt'st thou here?

Light. If you mistrust me, I'll be gone, my lord.

K. Edw. No, no; for, if thou mean'st to murder me,
Thou wilt return again; and therefore stay. [*Sleeps.*

Light. He sleeps.

K. Edw. [*waking*] O, let me not die yet! O, stay a while!

Light. How now, my lord!

K. Edw. Something still buzzeth in mine ears,
And tells me, if I sleep, I never wake:
This fear is that which makes me tremble thus;
And therefore tell me, wherefore art thou come?

Light. To rid thee of thy life.—Matrevis, come!

Enter MATREVIS *and* GURNEY.

K. Edw. I am too weak and feeble to resist. —
Assist me, sweet God, and receive my soul!

Light. Run for the table.

K. Edw. O, spare me, or despatch me in a trice!
[*Matrevis brings in a table. King Edward is murdered
by holding him down on the bed with the table, and

stamping on it.*

Light. So, lay the table down, and stamp on it,
But not too hard, lest that you bruise his body.

Mat. I fear me that this cry will raise the town,
And therefore let us take horse and away.

Light. Tell me, sirs, was it not bravely done?

Gur. Excellent well: take this for thy reward.
[*Stabs Lightborn, who dies.*
Come, let us cast the body in the moat,
And bear the king's to Mortimer our lord:
Away!

[*Exeunt with the bodies.*

SCENE VI. WESTMINSTER, A ROOM IN THE PALACE.

Enter the younger MORTIMER *and* MATREVIS.

Y. Mor. Is't done, Matrevis, and the murderer dead?

Mat. Ay, my good lord: I would it were undone!

Y. Mor. Matrevis, if thou now grow'st penitent,
I'll be thy ghostly father; therefore choose,
Whether thou wilt be secret in this,
Or else die by the hand of Mortimer.

Mat. Gurney, my lord, is fled, and will, I fear,
Betray us both; therefore let me fly.

Y. Mor. Fly to the savages!

Mat. I humbly thank your honour. [*Exit.*

Y. Mor. As for myself, I stand as Jove's huge tree,
And others are but shrubs compar'd to me:
All tremble at my name, and I fear none:
Let's see who dare impeach me for his death!

Enter QUEEN ISABELLA.

Q. Isab. Ah, Mortimer, the king my son hath news,
His father's dead, and we have murder'd him!

Y. Mor. What if he have? the king is yet a child.

Q. Isab. Ay, but he tears his hair, and wrings his hands,
And vows to be reveng'd upon us both.
Into the council-chamber he is gone,
To crave the aid and succour of his peers.
Ay me, see where he comes, and they with him!
Now, Mortimer, begins our tragedy.

Enter KING EDWARD THE THIRD, Lords, *and* Attendants.

First Lord. Fear not, my lord; know that you are a king.

K. Edw. Third. Villain!—

Y. Mor. Ho, now, my lord!

K. Edw. Third. Think not that I am frighted with thy words:

My father's murder'd through thy treachery;
And thou shalt die, and on his mournful hearse
Thy hateful and accursed head shall lie,
To witness to the world that by thy means
His kingly body was too soon interr'd.

Q. Isab. Weep not, sweet son.

K. Edw. Third. Forbid not me to weep; he was my father;
And had you lov'd him half so well as I,
You could not bear his death thus patiently:
But you, I fear, conspir'd with Mortimer.

First Lord. Why speak you not unto my lord the king?

Y. Mor. Because I think scorn to be accus'd.
Who is the man dares say I murder'd him?

K. Edw. Third. Traitor, in me my loving father speaks,
And plainly saith, 'twas thou that murder'dst him.

Y. Mor. But hath your grace no other proof than this? *K. Edw. Third.* Yes, if
this be the hand of Mortimer.

[*Showing letter.*

Y. Mor. False Gurney hath betray'd me and himself.

[*Aside to Queen Isabella.*

Q. Isab. I fear'd as much: murder can not be hid.

Y. Mor. It is my hand; what gather you by this?

K. Edw. Third. That thither thou didst send a murderer.

Y. Mor. What murderer? bring forth the man I sent.

K. Edw. Third. Ah, Mortimer, thou know'st that he is slain!
And so shalt thou be too.—Why stays he here?
Bring him unto a hurdle, drag him forth;
Hang him, I say, and set his quarters up:
And bring his head back presently to me.

Q. Isab. For my sake, sweet son, pity Mortimer!

Y. Mor. Madam, entreat not: I will rather die Than sue for life unto a paltry
boy.

K. Edw. Third. Hence with the traitor, with the murderer!

Y. Mor. Base Fortune, now I see, that in thy wheel
There is a point, to which when men aspire,
They tumble headlong down: that point I touch'd,
And, seeing there was no place to mount up higher,
Why should I grieve at my declining fall?—
Farewell, fair queen: weep not for Mortimer,
That scorns the world, and, as a traveller,

Goes to discover countries yet unknown.

K. Edw. Third. What, suffer you the traitor to delay?

[*Exit the younger Mortimer with First Lord and some of the Attendants.*

Q. Isab. As thou receivest thy life from me,
Spill not the blood of gentle Mortimer!

K. Edw. Third. This argues that you spilt my father's blood,
Else would you not entreat for Mortimer.

Q. Isab. I spill his blood! no.

K. Edw. Third. Ay, madam, you; for so the rumour runs.

Q. Isab. That rumour is untrue: for loving thee,
Is this report rais'd on poor Isabel.

K. Edw. Third. I do not think her so unnatural.

Sec. Lord. My lord, I fear me it will prove too true.

K. Edw. Third. Mother, you are suspected for his death
And therefore we commit you to the Tower,
Till further trial may be made thereof.
If you be guilty, though I be your son,
Think not to find me slack or pitiful.

Q. Isab. Nay, to my death; for too long have I liv'd,
Whenas my son thinks to abridge my days.

K. Edw. Third. Away with her! her words enforce these tears,
And I shall pity her, if she speak again.

Q. Isab. Shall I not mourn for my beloved lord?
And with the rest accompany him to his grave.

Sec. Lord. Thus, madam, 'tis the king's will you shall hence.

Q. Isab. He hath forgotten me: stay; I am his mother.

Sec. Lord. That boots not; therefore, gentle madam, go.

Q. Isab. Then come, sweet death, and rid me of this grief!

[*Exit with Second Lord and some of the Attendants.*

Re-enter First Lord, *with the head of the younger* MORTIMER.

First Lord. My lord, here is the head of Mortimer.

K. Edw. Third Go fetch my father's hearse, where it shall lie;
And bring my funeral robes. [*Exeunt Attendants.*
Accursed head,
Could I have rul'd thee then, as I do now,
Thou hadst not hatch'd this monstrous treachery!—
Here comes the hearse: help me to mourn, my lords.

Re-enter Attendants, *with the hearse and funeral robes.*

Sweet father, here unto thy murder'd ghost
I offer up the wicked traitor's head;
And let these tears, distilling from mine eyes,
Be witness of my grief and innocency.

[*Exeunt.*

Lector House believes that a society develops through a two-fold approach of continuous learning and adaptation, which is derived from the study of classic literary works spread across the historic timeline of literature records. Therefore, we aim at reviving, repairing and redeveloping all those inaccessible or damaged but historically as well as culturally important literature across subjects so that the future generations may have an opportunity to study and learn from past works to embark upon a journey of creating a better future.

This book is a result of an effort made by Lector House towards making a contribution to the preservation and repair of original ancient works which might hold historical significance to the approach of continuous learning across subjects.

HAPPY READING & LEARNING!

LECTOR HOUSE LLP
E-MAIL: lectorpublishing@gmail.com

9 789353 424237

Printed in July 2019
by Rotomail Italia S.p.A., Vignate (MI) - Italy